© Kevin Knight/theshutterclick.com

About the Author

LESLIE SIMON, coauthor of *Everybody Hurts: An Essential Guide to Emo Culture,* is a senior editor at Buzzent.com. Her work has appeared in *Kerrang!* and *Alternative Press.* She lives in Los Angeles, California, where she is determined to stalk Michael Cera until he marries her—or he's forced to get a restraining order. Whichever happens first.

**ALSO BY LESLIE SIMON
AND TREVOR KELLEY**
*Everybody Hurts:
An Essential Guide to Emo Culture*

WiSH YOU WERE HERE

An Essential Guide to Your Favorite
Music Scenes—from Punk to Indie
and Everything in Between

LESLIE SIMON
With Contributions by TREVOR KELLEY

Illustrations by ROB DOBI

HARPER

NEW YORK ● LONDON ● TORONTO ● SYDNEY

HARPER

HarperCollins books may be purchased for educational, business, or sales promotional use. For information please write: Special Markets Department, HarperCollins Publishers, 10 East 53rd Street, New York, NY 10022.

FIRST EDITION

Designed by Justin Dodd

Library of Congress Cataloging-in-Publication Data is available upon request.

ISBN 978-0-06-157371-2

09 10 11 12 13 OV/RRD 10 9 8 7 6 5 4 3 2 1

Contents

It's been nearly two years since *Everybody Hurts: An Essential Guide to Emo Culture* hit bookstore shelves and a lot has happened to your beloved authors since then. The flannel-loving Mr. Trevor Kelley snagged an amazing full-time job with MySpace, hoofed it to Los Angeles, and recently married his cuter-than-cute soul mate. I, on the other hand, left my post at *Alternative Press* magazine, accepted an amazing gig as senior editor at Buzznet.com, and made the big move to L.A., too—all while spending much of my nonexistent free time fighting off the advances of numerous suitors who insisted on showering me with lavish gifts like G5 jets and expensive bottles of Perrier-Jouët Belle Epoque champagne. (Note to future admirers: No money man can win my love, Neneh Cherry–style. Just sayin'.)

Somewhere amidst all the moves, marriages, and million-dollar acts of adoration, I managed to pen our emo bible's follow-up, which is what you happen to be holding in your hot little hands. When I set out to write *Wish You Were Here: An Essential Guide to Your Favorite Music Scenes—from Punk to Indie and Everything in Between*, I wanted to achieve the following objectives: (1) to speak to music fans outside the emo echelon and prove I could write about more than just Gabe Saporta and guyliner, (2) to compile a collection of the most cherished music scenes out there in these here United States and offer up witty and insightful observations on said soundscapes, and (3) to come up with a title that was almost as much of a mouthful as the name of Fiona Apple's sophomore album.* Judging from the end result, I'd have to say mission accomplished on all three counts.

What follows is an eleven-city tour of what I consider to be the most influential and awe-inspiring music scenes in existence today. In addition to covering all corners of the map—from the Pacific Northwest to the Sunshine State—*Wish You Were Here* also dishes the dirt surrounding your favorite bands' stomping grounds. In each chapter, you'll be given a history lesson on the bands that cultivated the community and the groups that are keeping the scene alive today. You'll also be given a directory of must-see points of interest that you can't find in any Fodor's travel guide. Want to know where Henry Rollins used to scoop fro-yo in Washington, D.C., back when he still had hair—and a neck? Got it covered. Eager to figure out the best place in Los Angeles to watch Jenny Lewis run suicide sprints? That's a no brainer.

Don't get it twisted, though. *Wish You Were Here* isn't a travel guide. No way. If anything, it's more like a musical ethnography, which is why I've also included other elements like essential album guides, untold stories behind some of the scenes' most groundbreaking record labels, and a ton of features intended to boost your musical IQ at least a couple of points. (Don't believe me? Well, thanks to special scene excavation technology, I've unearthed plenty of insider information so even the most diehard fans can learn a thing or two. Swears!)

Finally, before anyone starts spewing Haterade in my general di-

---

* *When the Pawn Hits the Conflicts He Thinks Like a King What He Knows Throws the Blows When He Goes to the Fight and He'll Win the Whole Thing 'Fore He Enters the Ring There's No Body to Batter When Your Mind Is Your Might so When You Go Solo, You Hold Your Own Hand and Remember That Depth Is the Greatest of Heights and If You Know Where You Stand, Then You Know Where to Land and If You Fall It Won't Matter, Cuz You'll Know That You're Right*

rection because their favorite music scene isn't represented in these here pages, put down the shaving shears and umbrella, Britney. I'm sure a place like Crib Death, Iowa, has a really kick-ass local music community, but I just couldn't cut down that many trees to make the necessary page count this time around. However, that's not to say that you couldn't find me pimping your preferred scene sometime soon. Stay tuned!

—Leslie Simon
September 2008

1987

Though they disbanded the year before, Embrace releases its self-titled debut on Dischord Records and posthumously becomes one of the first emo bands on record. The same year, former Embrace and Minor Threat guitarist/vocalist Ian MacKaye forms Fugazi, which is widely embraced by fans and critics alike and eventually sets the standard for what we now consider the musical genre of post-hardcore.

Washington, D.C.

When discussing the scenes that helped shape the underground as we know it, there's no better place to start than Washington, D.C., the birthplace of "emo" and the current home to a whole lot of crotchety scene vets.

MUSIC PRIMER

When you're talking D.C.'s long and storied history, you have to start with the hardcore movement that began there in the early '80s. Most locals will agree that this particular sub-faction kicked off with **Bad Brains**, hands down one of the best, weirdest, and most dangerous punk bands ever to play hardcore music. (For example, when they were recording their third album *I Against I*, Paul "H.R." Hudson was in jail and ended up recording the vocals for "Sacred Love" through a pay phone near his cell.) Understandably, this was the kind of band that either scared the crap out of you or inspired you to form a group just like it, which explains why a slew of hyperactive punk bands began popping up in the D.C. scene not long after Bad Brains formed.

One of the most notable acts to follow in their footsteps was **Minor Threat**, another groundbreaking hardcore band whom many credit for bringing attention to the underground "straight edge"*

---

* *n.* A lifestyle in which one abstains from drinking, drugs, and a bunch of other fun things Minor Threat preached about. In the early '80s, thousands of soda-drinking

scene and for inciting, well, a whole lot of suburban middle-class teenagers to beat the snot out of each other anytime the band played locally. Seeing as how most sane people prefer to perform without some dude's elbow lodged in their esophagus, it wasn't long before Minor Threat singer Ian MacKaye and many of his contemporaries began experimenting with genres of music that were less likely to incite a riot. Whereas the members of Bad Brains became Rastafarians and released an album full of reggae songs, Minor Threat broke up, sparking MacKaye to form **Embrace**, a new post-hardcore group that became known for combining melodic rock structures with lyrics about such masculine topics as, uh, playing dress-up and crying.

These days, most people would consider Embrace to be an emo band. But at the time, MacKaye and another early D.C. emo band, **Rites of Spring**, were actually paving new ground, and they continued to do so in the late '80s when MacKaye—along with two members of Rites of Spring and a bass player who looked like Christopher Walken—formed **Fugazi**, quite possibly the most fiercely respected D.C. punk band on the planet. The band quickly earned their rep by employing a number of strict band policies, which included playing only five-dollar shows, discouraging fans from slam-dancing, and re-

teenagers flocked to D.C. in order to truly live the straight-edge lifestyle, only to realize they were robbing themselves of all things that normal teenagers are *supposed* to do. That said, you won't find many in D.C. who are still straight edge—well, except for Ian MacKaye, who could probably use a drink more than anyone.

fusing to sell any merchandise (except their infamous "This Is Not a Fugazi T-shirt" T-shirt).

Considering that these days most mainstream punk bands have their own clothing line, brand of energy drink, and Proactiv endorsement contract (*cough*—Cute Is What We Aim For—*cough*), this was a pretty altruistic* way of doing things. However, over the next few years, many in the D.C. scene rebelled against it by signing to major labels in order to pay for lavish things like heat and rent. Two local and experimental post-hardcore bands, **Jawbox** and **Shudder to Think**, both signed to majors at the time, but neither of them exactly connected with a larger audience—although, the latter of the two did turn up on an episode of *Beavis and Butthead* in which the cartooned couch crusaders referred to the flamboyant lead singer Craig Wedren as a "butt munch."

After a few years of middling record sales, both Jawbox and Shudder to Think broke up and the D.C. scene went through yet another musical transformation. This time, the locals started churning out a unique style of angular rock that was somehow danceable. But what else would

---

* *n*. A word that air-quote "artists" use when they are trying to impress other people at gallery openings and vegan potlucks.

you expect from a bunch of pasty white dudes who looked like they spent the better part of their teen years sequestered to their bedroom, eagerly studying for the AP calculus test or fearful of a polymorphic light eruption?* First came **the Dismemberment Plan**, a group of guys so nerdy that they once wrote a song about getting it on while watching CNN. (That'd be "Ellen and Ben," off their 2001 album *Change*, in case you were wondering.) Later, they were followed by **Q and Not U**, a quasi-dance punk group that named itself after an obscure Scrabble rule.† And, more recently, **Georgie James** entered the scene, playing the type of hyperactive indie-pop that your typical yuppie thirtysomething would listen to on the way to Sunday brunch at First Watch.

Since the turn of the millennium, the D.C. scene has evolved into something a little less under-the-radar. Sure, you still have mainstays like MacKaye churning out new bands (like **the Evens**, an indie-rock duo he formed with his wife, former **Warmers** drummer Amy Farina), but fans seem to be more impressed by accessibility these days. Self-centered pop-rock bands like **Army of Me** and **You, Me, and Everyone We Know** seem to be the order of the day, followed by death-metal enthusiasts **Darkest Hour** and the sunny Christian rockers in **Mae** (which hail from neighboring Arlington, Virginia). That said, if there's one thing that's remained consistent in the D.C. music scene over the past thirty years, it's got to be diversity.

LABEL CONSCIOUS

Ah, **Dischord Records**—linchpin of the D.C. punk and post-hardcore scene. Started by **Teen Idles** bandmates (and former Wilson

---

* *n.* Medical condition in which a rash or series of blisters is brought on by prolonged exposure to the sun. This disorder generally occurs in females aged twenty to forty and in 90 percent of people who attend Comic-Con.

† There are actually twenty-four words that do *not* follow the usual *q*-is-always-followed-by-*u* spelling rule. For a full list, please consult your trusty *Official Scrabble Players Dictionary*.

High School classmates) Ian MacKaye and Jeff Nelson, Dischord was originally created as a way for the teens to release their band's album *Minor Disturbance*. However, it wasn't long before other local acts, impressed by the label's DIY ethic, also wanted to put out their albums through Dischord.

After running the label out of their bedrooms, MacKaye and Nelson moved the label headquarters to Arlington, Virginia, in 1981, soon occupied a bungalow they christened Dischord House, and started putting out albums by **Void**, **Scream**, **Rites of Spring**, **Dag Nasty**, and **Fugazi**, among others. In the late '80s, the label launched Dischord Direct, an in-house distribution service that helped other local bands and labels (like DeSoto and Lovitt) get their albums in stores. Dischord then reaped the benefits of the '90s alt-rock boom and garnered a lot of media attention for launching the careers of **Jawbox** and **Shudder to Think**, both of which eventually signed with major labels and released albums the mainstream music-buying public could've cared less about. Unfazed, Dischord continued to do what they did best: Put out great records by underground D.C. bands like **Channels**, **Q and Not U**, and **Lungfish**. Over the past twenty-five-plus years, Dischord Records has had its shares of ups and downs—musically, financially, and politically—but the label has always managed to persevere and prosper. Like I always say, "After a nuclear holocaust, all that will be left are cockroaches and Dischord Records."

ESSENTIAL WASHINGTON, D.C., ALBUM GUIDE

Now that you've properly educated yourself about the scene's history, it's time to go out and buy every damn album this scene has churned out. The list below should not only provide the average newcomer with a good starting-off point, but it should also arm know-it-all scenesters with some pretty impressive info they can spew out very loudly at the next local show.

RITES OF SPRING: *RITES OF SPRING* (DISCHORD, 1985)

WHAT YOU NEED TO KNOW: As arguably the first emo band ever, Rites of Spring was far more sentimental than most of its D.C. peers. In fact, it's still incredibly impressive that singer Guy Picciotto would perform songs like "Theme (If I Started Crying)" at punk clubs in D.C. without someone giving him a wedgie.

WHAT TO TELL THE LOCALS: The next time someone brings up a new-school emo band like the Maine, you might want to respond with, "If Guy could hear what people are calling 'emo' now, he would roll over in his grave." Then quickly excuse yourself, before someone points out that Picciotto is, in fact, still alive.

EMBRACE: *EMBRACE* (DISCHORD, 1987)

WHAT YOU NEED TO KNOW: Along with Rites of Spring, Embrace is another D.C. band credited for kick-starting the emo movement. This is the only album the band released and it marks the only occasion in Ian MacKaye's career in which he felt comfortable writing love songs that didn't involve ridiculously vague metaphors about Coca-Cola.

WHAT TO TELL THE LOCALS: You could definitely score some points for saying that, after an exhaustive YouTube search, you found footage of the Embrace show in the mid-'80s where someone yelled, "What are you guys? *Emo*-core?" and unintentionally named one of the most argued about genres of all time.

FUGAZI: *REPEATER* (DISCHORD, 1988)

WHAT YOU NEED TO KNOW: After both Rites of Spring and Embrace broke up, Picciotto and MacKaye formed Fugazi, arguably the most respected punk band of all time. Prior to the release of this album, practically every sleazy major-label A&R executive in the world tried to sign the group. You can probably guess how this turned out.

WHAT TO TELL THE LOCALS: Considering that it may have been the greatest song about selling T-shirts ever written, you might want to

<9>

suggest that the fourth track on this album, "Merchandise," changed your "outlook on the ethics of art and commerce." Just make sure you're not wearing that bootleg *Repeater* cover art T-shirt you bought on eBay when you do so.

MINOR THREAT: *COMPLETE DISCOGRAPHY* (DISCHORD, 1989)

WHAT YOU NEED TO KNOW: Before laying the groundwork for the D.C. scene with their label, Dischord Records, Ian MacKaye and Jeff Nelson played in the pioneering punk group Minor Threat. This album contains the band's entire body of work, including "Steppin' Stone," perhaps the only acceptable cover of a Monkees song ever.

WHAT TO TELL THE LOCALS: Though you'll rarely hear a bad word spoken about them, you can definitely earn some scene points for claiming that it "crushed a small piece of your soul" when Nike used the cover of this album in a series of "edgy" print ads.*

NATION OF ULYSSES: *PLAYS PRETTY FOR BABY* (DISCHORD, 1992)

WHAT YOU NEED TO KNOW: In the early '90s, there were very few groups as unconventional as Nation of Ulysses. (Two words: Trumpet player. Enough said.) After all, this was a band that referred to itself as a "political party," published nonsensical fanzines and, on the cover of this album, looked like Mormon missionaries. No, seriously.

WHAT TO TELL THE LOCALS: Honestly, no one from the D.C. scene would ever understate the continued influence of Nation of Ulysses on the future of post-hardcore. And, seeing that there con-

---

* The short-lived ad campaign was used for the Major Threat skateboarding tour and featured a seated look-alike wearing a pair of Nikes instead of combat boots. When Ian MacKaye got wind of the posters, he threatened legal action and encouraged all Minor Threat fans to organize a letter-writing campaign protesting the shoe giant. Soon after, Nike apologized and destroyed all future promotional material.

tinue to be bands that have made a successful living out of ripping off the quintet's unique fashion sense and high-energy live shows (the Hives, anyone?), I anticipate that the band will continue to inspire the shape of post-hardcore to come.

GIRLS AGAINST BOYS: *VENUS LUXURE NO. 1 BABY* **(TOUCH AND GO, 1993)**

WHAT YOU NEED TO KNOW: Chances are, you probably don't associate looking like a male model, drinking martinis, or getting laid with being part of a D.C. post-hardcore band. Yet, when Girls Against Boys released this album, they somehow became known for all three.

WHAT TO TELL THE LOCALS: That you love (nay, worship) the records that Girls Against Boys made before they left D.C. for New York in the early '90s. Whatever you do, don't bring up the fact that they earned a paycheck a few years ago by serving as the backing band for *Showgirls* star Gina Gershon. I'm sure they're embarrassed enough for the both of you.

JAWBOX: *FOR YOUR OWN SPECIAL SWEETHEART* (ATLANTIC, 1994)

WHAT YOU NEED TO KNOW: When Jawbox signed to a major label to make this record in the early '90s, many in the D.C. scene cried foul. Fifteen years later, *For Your Own Special Sweetheart* is considered a classic and many of those original haters have realized they're far too old to care about "selling out" anyways—especially when they're too busy punching their time card at Guitar Center.

WHAT TO TELL THE LOCALS: After Jawbox called it a day, vocalist/guitarist J. Robbins became one of the most ubiquitous—not to mention affordable—indie producers around after working on albums by the Promise Ring, None More Black, and Murder by Death. That said, you can probably claim that the dude recorded your band's first album, and chances are, you won't actually be lying.

SHUDDER TO THINK: *PONY EXPRESS RECORD* (EPIC, 1994)

WHAT YOU NEED TO KNOW: Like Jawbox, Shudder to Think jumped to the majors to record this album, which was pretty much overlooked by most of the record-buying public. You might be hard-pressed to find this masterpiece in the average fan's iTunes playlist, but the album remains a blueprint for any post-hardcore band that wants to see its bright, shiny face on *FNMTV*.

WHAT TO TELL THE LOCALS: If you have ever even remotely thought about shaving your head, wearing dramatic eye shadow, and singing like an opera singer over a bunch of art-rock skronking,* then you should definitely tell people that Wedren is your "muse."

---

* *n.* A style of music that is grating, avant-garde, and totally hard to listen to—unless you have a degree in music synthesis from the Berklee College of Music.

THE DISMEMBERMENT PLAN: *EMERGENCY & I* (DESOTO, 1999)

WHAT YOU NEED TO KNOW: In the late '90s, emo was becoming more and more of a buzz term, and after a few tours opening for then-rising stars like the Promise Ring and Death Cab for Cutie, the Dismemberment Plan signed to Interscope to record this artsy punk album. Many in the D.C. scene would grow to love it. As for the new label? Yeah, not so much.

WHAT TO TELL THE LOCALS: Interscope eventually dropped the Dismemberment Plan and *Emergency & I* was later released on a local indie label, where it became a cult favorite. In the future, you should definitely insist that every mix CD you make includes "The City," one of the catchiest singles Interscope never released.

Q AND NOT U: *NO KILL NO BEEP BEEP* (DISCHORD, 2000)

WHAT YOU NEED TO KNOW: By the late '90s, the D.C. scene had gone from brainy post-hardcore to danceable punk rock, and in the midst of this transition, a couple of fanzine editors formed Q and Not U. Their goal? To write songs for house parties—and for those who need things spelled out, there's a picture of them playing *at* a house party on the cover of this record.

WHAT TO TELL THE LOCALS: Definitely suggest that, after going back and buying this album, some of the esoteric lyrics singer Chris Richards wrote often made you consult Dictionary.com.

TED LEO/PHARMACISTS: *HEARTS OF OAK* (LOOKOUT!, 2003)

WHAT YOU NEED TO KNOW: In the early 2000s, D.C. scenester Ted Leo watched dumbfounded as his music became a staple on MTV and critics' best-of lists. As a result, several major labels began courting the former Chisel frontman. In true D.C. fashion, he told them all to go sit and spin.

WHAT TO TELL THE LOCALS: You should definitely tell anyone in D.C. that you can totally relate to Ted's "moral fiber." After all, not only does the guy dress like a Bible salesman, but he's also a strict vegan and political activist. More important, Leo proved that it was okay for indie-rock listeners to fall in love with Kelly Clarkson after his unexpected cover of "Since U Been Gone" became an online phenomenon.

HOW TO PROPERLY IDENTIFY A D.C. PUNK BAND

Thanks to this handy-dandy list, you should have at least a hundred hours of music to program on your MP3 player. After you're done importing the tunage, it's important to get to know D.C. bands on an aesthetic level. To do that, I suggest you take a look at the scenarios below. I'm betting if you encounter any of the following situations, then you're definitely in the presence of a bona fide D.C. punk band—and, more than likely, a disciple of scene consigliere Ian MacKaye.

UPON ARRIVING AT THE CLUB, YOU PAY THE PRICE OF ADMISSION, AND TO YOUR SURPRISE, IT COSTS LESS THAN SEEING THE LATEST WILL FERRELL FLICK.

Thanks to MacKaye and his penny-pinching ways, many D.C. bands have made it a point to keep ticket prices around five dollars *and* require that shows remain all-ages. Supposedly, the reason most local acts do this is because they believe it further breaks down the divide between the artist and the fans, establishes intergenerational equity,[*] and attempts to offer audiences a shot at popular sovereignty.[†] In reality, cheap ticket prices give otherwise broke-ass mofos the opportunity to experience good music without risking overdraft charges from their checking account. How do I know? Because most musicians in D.C. bands *are* a bunch of broke-ass mofos who are all too familiar with accumulating a shit-ton of overdraft charges on their checking account. It's called "pay it forward." Look into it.

---

[*] The novel concept of fairness between children and adults.

[†] The even *more* novel concept of creating a government in which people are the source of all political power.

ONCE INSIDE, YOU NOTICE THE BAND IS NOT PLAYING ON THE STAGE—BUT ON THE SPACE *IN FRONT* OF THE STAGE.

For just about as long as anyone can remember, bands in the D.C. scene have frequently chosen to play on the floor of a club. Part of this acts as a nod to the good ol' days when Fugazi would play shows in a dingy basement or dilapidated youth center. (It's interesting to note, though, that Fugazi eventually grew far too popular for such miniscule venues and graduated to the kind of nightclubs that were known to have professional lighting and—*shudder*—an actual doorman. *Shhhh* . . . Don't tell the purists!)

Keeping that in mind, when a band sets up in front of the stage these days, it probably means one of two things: (1) This is a group that will not under any circumstance submit to the confines of a typical and subservient rock band, which were totally set up by "the man," who is undoubtedly part of the evil establishment; and (2) this is a group that will spend the next hour feverishly sweating on any poor bastard standing in the front row. And for that, I recommend you don't leave home without an umbrella . . . ella, ella. Eh, eh, eh.

ONCE THE BAND STARTS ITS SET, IT BECOMES APPARENT THAT THE LEAD SINGER IS SUFFERING FROM AN UNCONTROLLABLE CASE OF VERBAL DIARRHEA.

When seeing a D.C. punk act, there will inevitably come a time when the band's lead singer will stop the set and, without any irony, begin rambling on and on about whatever it is that's currently troubling him. Looking back, Fugazi may also be to blame for this. After all, this is the same band that allowed Ian MacKaye to talk endlessly at its live shows about pressing political and social issues like racism, sexism, and consumerism. While this didn't stop frat boys everywhere from forming a circle pit anytime the band played "Waiting Room," it did inspire many local groups to begin spitting out boring diatribes at their own live shows, resulting in God knows how many completely unnecessary and self-important rants about the possibility of rising transport costs altering world trade, the latest bombing spree in China, or how well Tide to Go stick really *does* work at getting out stains—like the Taco Bell fire sauce the lead singer spilled all over his white Hanes undershirt while scarfing down a Chalupa Baja before the gig. Who needs the educated and eloquent correspondents at CNN when you can get all your news from a dude who thinks outside the bun?

AFTER THE BAND FINSHES ITS SET, THE HOUSE LIGHTS TURN ON AND YOUR EARS ARE SUDDENLY ACCOSTED BY THE BOOM OF STEEL DRUMS

This may seem a little strange, initially, but do your research and you'll see that there has been a longtime love affair between D.C. bands and Jamaican dudes. The first band to embrace this was Bad Brains, who just so happened to be a bunch of reggae-loving Rastafarians. Then came—*wait for it*—Fugazi, who incorporated touches of the island-based genre on its 1993 album *In on the Kill Taker*. Finally, it wasn't too long ago that former D.C. native Ted Leo celebrated his love for all things ska with the song "Where Have All the Rude Boys* Gone?" But whatever, we'll let that slide.

The point here is, much like those D.C. stalwarts, the current scene is still very fond of reggae, so don't be alarmed if you hear Fela Kuti being played over the loud speakers as you head toward the door. Instead, you might as well give Afrobeat a chance, because you never know when the rhythm is gonna get you, Miami Sound Machine-

* *n.* Juvenile delinquents associated with the poorest area of Kingston, Jamaica, in the 1960s. The term then evolved in the 1970s to describe British youths who were fans of ska music and the surrounding street culture.

style. One minute, you're sitting around with your friends, dissecting Lungfish lyrics, and the next, you're heeding the call of the red, yellow, and gold by burning Nag Champa incense and backcombing dreadlocks into your hair. It's a slippery slope, so proceed with caution. After all, there's a fine line between hanging up a Reggae Boyz* poster flag and joining Trenchtown Rock, your local Bob Marley tribute band.

ON YOUR WAY OUT, YOU SPOT WHAT LOOKS LIKE SOMEONE'S GRANDFATHER HANGING AROUND THE MERCH TABLE. UPON CLOSER INSPECTION, YOU REALIZE THE ELDERLY GENTLEMAN IS ACTUALLY THE BAND'S BASS PLAYER.

Let's face it: D.C. was once a young man's town. When you watch a documentary like *American Hardcore*, it's hard not to focus on how young everyone was. After all, back in the day, local punk kids were shaving their heads because they thought it looked badass—not because they were suffering from male-pattern baldness. Sucks to be human cue balls like Ian MacKaye and J. Robbins, huh? It's precisely for this reason that on any given night you may see the kind of guy who looks like a middle-aged physics teacher—or Dr. Keith Ablow— play in an angular rock band at a local club. Just like there's no age prerequisite to *see* a local show, there's also no age prerequisite to *play* one, either. That's the way it works in D.C.: Short of stroke, cardiac arrest, or acute renal failure, you're never too old to rock.

HOW TO KNOW WHEN YOU'VE BECOME A D.C. ELDER STATESMAN

Much like male-pattern baldness (mentioned above), memory loss is also something that happens when you start getting on in years. If you

* *n.* The Jamaican national football—*er*, soccer—team.

can't remember your middle name, the last four digits of your social security number, or the year Minor Threat called it quits, then there's a good chance you're a D.C. elder statesman. Still not sure if this section applies to you? Why not read on to determine if any of the following things are starting to occur in your life—or if you're on the verge of becoming totally senile.

✓ YOU LIVE IN MOUNT PLEASANT

In D.C., Mount Pleasant is where all aging scenesters go to die. Okay, they're probably *years* from kicking the bucket, but they definitely relocate here in order to retreat to a somewhat quiet life in suburbia. Spend more than fifteen minutes in the area and you're bound to run into some dude who used to be in a band on Dischord Records and now pushes a baby stroller and sips overpriced green tea lattes from Caribou Coffee. Yuppies unite!

✓ YOU PLAY IN A BAND, BUT YOU REFUSE TO TOUR

Just because you're older doesn't mean you've lost the desire to play distorted guitars or sing obtuse lyrics. However, you *have* stopped getting your kicks from being smooshed in a van with nine other smelly dudes and sleeping next to cat litter boxes on strangers' floors. (Go figure.) In fact, you'd rather spend your time watching *Pancake Mountain* with your kids, and I can't think of anything more punk-rock than that.

✓ YOU STILL GO TO SHOWS, DESPITE THE FACT THAT YOUR PRESENCE CREEPS PEOPLE OUT

As D.C. scenesters get older, they will at least try to stay in touch with the same community of bands that they grew up listening to. Maybe they'll buy the new Lungfish record or go see Chris Richards's new band at a house party in Arlington. While it's respectable and, in some ways, kind of cute that someone pushing forty would want to hang out in a basement with a bunch of sweaty kids, let's face it: At some point, someone at the aforementioned show will inevitably think, "Dude, who brought the narc?"

WASHINGTON, D.C.

<18>

✓ YOU'RE NOT STRAIGHT EDGE ANYMORE

Like I said earlier, no one in D.C. stays straight edge forever,* so don't feel *too* bad if you start craving a drink every now and again. That's not the issue here. No, the issue is this: For many in the D.C. scene, it becomes a rite of passage to begin hosting stuffy dinner parties at their new two-bedroom condos. At these parties, oftentimes a group of friends will sit around and talk about the latest Haruki Murakami book while drinking expensive red wine. Again, not a horrible thing in and of itself, but if you begin to tell your friends at such a gathering that the Shiraz you're serving has "a fantastic, earthy taste to it," take a minute to reflect, because there's a good chance you are *not* a D.C. elder statesmen. Nope, you're just plain old.

MAPPING OUT WASHINGTON D.C.

9:30 CLUB (930 F ST. NW, WASHINGTON, D.C. 20004; HTTP://WWW.930.COM)

Before moving to its current location, the original 9:30 Club was a lot like your typical VFW hall: The shows were all-ages, the set times were

---

* Except for Ian MacKaye, of course.

generally early, and it didn't cost a fortune to get in. One of the reasons for this is that it often smelled like a combination of rat piss, fresh vomit, cheap beer, hairspray, cigarettes, and musty leather. This isn't any sort of exaggeration, either. Just ask any D.C. scene vet and he or she will tell you the old 9:30 was by far the worst-smelling nightclub in the history of terrible-smelling nightclubs.

It's no wonder that the venue decided to move to a location that includes such posh accoutrements as air-conditioning and scented urinal mints. (Ah, heaven.) Over the years, this new space has become a proving ground for new-school pop-punk groups like Good Charlotte more than it has been a home for grizzled scene vets like Channels, but hey, tattooed millionaires who will one day knock up Lionel Richie's daughter gotta start somewhere, too.

BEN'S CHILI BOWL (1213 U ST. NW, WASHINGTON, D.C. 20009; HTTP://WWW.BENSCHILIBOWL.COM)

For the most part, D.C. is the kind of place where you end up riding your bike over to a friend's place in order to have a vegan potluck. But that's not to say that there isn't a string of dingy restaurants where you'll often find band dudes loitering. Ben's is definitely one of them, and for the past three decades, everyone from Be Your Own Pet to, uh,

Hillary Clinton has come here for a hearty bowl of beans before heading off to the next city in search of rock—and Pepto-Bismol.

THE BLACK CAT (1811 14TH ST. NW, WASHINGTON, D.C. 20009; HTTP://WWW.BLACKCATDC.COM)

It's a fact: No one can come to D.C. without spending at least one night at the Black Cat, by far the best all-ages rock club in all of D.C. Okay, maybe *some* people can, but usually those people have suffered a lobotomy and have bigger issues to deal with.

When the Black Cat originally opened its doors in the mid-'90s, it was seen as a pet project for mustache enthusiast and former D.C. scenester Dave Grohl. While the Foo Fighters' leader served as one of the Black Cat's many investors, he was hardly the only person calling the shots. In fact, during the early days, most of that responsibility lay squarely on the shoulders of Dante Ferrando, a lifelong D.C. scenester who, as a kid, used to stalk Black Flag's Henry Rollins and MacKaye at the Häagen-Dazs on M Street. By the time that he began running the show at the Black Cat, however, the D.C. music scene was going through a unquestionable period of transition: Many of the city's smaller venues were shutting down and old standbys like the 9:30 Club were moving into much larger digs on the other side of town. As a response to this, Ferrando decided to transform the Black Cat into the kind of large-scale rock club that still had the feel of a DIY punk show.

Essentially, the Black Cat is kind of like the club equivalent of *Cheers*—everyone here knows your name (but there are way more dudes wearing beanies).

DISCHORD HOUSE (2700-B N WASHINGTON BLVD., ARLINGTON, VA 22201)

Though it's a bit of a trek from D.C. proper, at some point you have to tap into your inner-stalker and drive by the Dischord House in Arlington, where you can still find Ian MacKaye answering the phone and filling mail orders to this day. Extra scene points for reenacting the photo from Minor Threat's *Salad Days* EP with your friends on the house's rickety front porch.

FORT RENO (3950 CHESAPEAKE ST. NW, WASHINGTON, D.C. 20016; HTTP://WWW.FORTRENO.COM)

One day in the late '80s, Mayor Marion Barry took time away from his busy schedule of smoking crack and buying hookers to help fund free summer concerts at this former Civil War battleground. In the time since, Fort Reno has become the destination spot for aging D.C. scenesters and, if you have ever wanted to see Joe Lally from Fugazi spooning soy yogurt into his daughter's mouth, well, that's kind of weird, but you can definitely do that here.

CROOKED BEAT RECORDS (2318 18TH ST. NW, WASHINGTON, D.C. 20009; HTTP://WWW.CROOKEDBEAT.COM)

There was once a time where it seemed like you couldn't go anywhere in the D.C. area without stumbling upon a kick-ass indie record store. Over the past ten years, both Now Music (located in nearby Arlington, Virginia) and Yesterday and Today (a quaint storefront owned by the dude who recorded Minor Threat's first 7-inch) have closed their doors, leaving many in the D.C. scene with nothing else to do but tip out their forties, gangsta rap–style, in their honor.* The only indie store that *didn't* get its ass capped in a drive-by, so to speak, was Crooked Beat, which remains one of the last safe havens for any record geek in the greater D.C. area and, perhaps more important, a reminder of how things used to be for music fans.

Throughout the store, you'll find rows of vinyl, a rack boasting D.C.-only releases, and, much like the Black Cat, the occasional local celebrity. In fact, try not to freak out if you see Ian Svenonius from Nation of Ulysses paying for a stack of Grand Funk Railroad LPs at the front counter—that's assuming you are one of the, say, four people who would actually recognize Svenonius if you saw him.

---

* Except for Ian MacKaye. He's still straight edge, remember?

HÄAGEN-DAZS (3120 M ST. NW, WASHINGTON, D.C. 20007; HTTP://WWW.HAAGEN-DAZS.COM)

When in town, you have to stop by the site of the famed ice-cream shop where MacKaye and Black Flag's Henry Rollins used to scoop up hot-fudge sundaes in exchange for wooden nickels—or, you know, whatever they were using for currency back when the two of them were actually teenagers.

HILLIARD FIELD (70 UNIVERSITY BLVD. E, SILVER SPRING, MD 20901)

Starting in the mid-'90s, the members of Jawbox, Shudder to Think, and Fugazi began a long-standing tradition of playing softball every Monday night at a field near a church in this suburban Maryland neighborhood. In true D.C. fashion, the loose-knit collective often made their own bases out of scraps of cardboard and stopped each inning to lecture onlookers about the evils of signing to a major label. Okay, I made the major label thing up, but it could've happened.

THE RAVEN GRILL (3125 MOUNT PLEASANT ST. NW, WASHINGTON, D.C. 20010)

Yet another staple in Mount Pleasant, the Raven Grill was *the* D.C. scene's dive bar of choice around the time that Svenonius posed on the cover of *Sassy*. (Try Google image searching *that*!) Fortunately, the dingy spot hasn't changed too much with the neighborhood: They still refuse to install an ATM inside and local punks continue to scrawl things like "If you took a cab here, you don't belong" on the bathroom walls.

WILSON CENTER (15TH ST. NW AND IRVING ST. NW, WASHINGTON, D.C. 20010)

Along with Wilson High (see below) and Fort Reno, this long-standing venue creates a trifecta of punk landmarks in northwest D.C., and no tour of the area is complete without it. Wilson is both where Fugazi played its first show and where Bad Brains threw down many of its most raucous sets. The next time you get stuck behind some elder statesmen at the 9:30 Club, you can bet the house they'll be loudly reminiscing about one of the supposedly historic shows that took place at Wilson.

WILSON HIGH SCHOOL (3950 CHESAPEAKE ST. NW, WASHINGTON, D.C. 20016; HTTP://WWW.WILSONHS.ORG)

In the late '70s and early '80s, this place was like the punk-rock version of *Fame*—minus the fuchsia leg warmers and students spontaneously bursting into song. Instead, many of the scholars here formed hardcore bands like Bad Brains (whose members were in the class of '78) and Minor Threat (whose frontman Ian MacKaye met drummer Jeff

WASHINGTON, D.C.

<24>

Nelson in German class; the two were soon writing songs about how much drinking sucked, despite the fact they couldn't legally step foot in a bar for another couple years).

A MOMENT OF SILENCE

D.C. SPACE (7TH ST. NW AND E ST. NW, WASHINGTON, D.C. 20004)

Back in the day, D.C. Space was actually a real-deal art gallery whose owners, in a momentary lapse of reason, agreed to let rowdy punk bands like Born Against play among the rows of paintings and black-and-white photographs that regularly lined the walls. Though you can probably imagine how that turned out, for a while D.C. Space was every bit as beloved as the old 9:30 Club, primarily because it was smaller and located a few blocks away.

What that meant for the local scene at the time was that, on any given night, you could see *two* bands at the same time. This was, apparently, a really big deal to people who lived in D.C. After all, how many people can say they were able to see Fugazi *and* Circus Lupus[*] play on the same day in 1993? I'm guessing not many. In addition to proximity, D.C. Space was also known for some pretty raucous performances. When you walked into the club, you never knew if you were going to end up on camera (like for Minor Threat's *DC Space/Buff Hall/9:30 Club* DVD) or end up getting puked on (as was the case with 9353 vocalist Bruce Merkle and a couple of unfortunate concertgoers). Luckily, not knowing what to expect was half the fun. Incidentally, D.C. Space was gutted a few years ago and turned into a Starbucks—just what the world needs more of.

---

[*] Hell, I don't know who Circus Lupus is, either, but being able to brag about seeing two shows in one night *is* pretty impressive—regardless of who the bands are.

May 10, 1994

Weezer releases its self-titled debut album, nick-named "The Blue Album" by fans. Thanks to its geek-chic look and songs like "Undone—The Sweater Song," the band would inadvertently go on to inspire thousands of nerdy guys living on the east side of Hollywood who dreamed of one day playing in a power-pop band of their own—and scoring a bunch of Asian chicks.

Los Ángeles, California

<27>

Like Washington, D.C., Los Angeles has long been an underground music Mecca. But what has the City of Angels contributed to the scene lately? How about a bunch of child actors and Scientologists who have formed some of the most widely adored indie-rock bands around.

MUSIC PRIMER

When you ponder the history of L.A.'s music scene, does it make you think about some brain-dead rock star's lengthy account of how he used to snort pounds of Bolivian cocaine while leading tantric sex sessions at his Malibu mansion? If so, then you have just purchased the wrong book.* Assuming you're not into that type of thing (and, really, unless you are forty-five years old and the better part of your body is made up of silicone and Restylane, why would you be?) there is an entirely different musical history in Los Angeles that's worth discussing here.

That history begins in the early '90s with artists such as Beck Hansen (that's **Beck**, if you're nasty), who began making a name for himself by playing at sketchy clubs like the Jabberjaw (see "A Moment of Silence"), which, no joke, was located in Compton. At the time, Beck was far from famous and not only did he sell his music on hand-dubbed

---

* The right book being, of course, *Don't Try This at Home* by Dave Navarro. But, hey, there's a pretty good chance that you can contract an STD by just picking that thing up at your local Barnes & Noble. Don't say I didn't warn you.

cassettes, but he also rode around the city on an MTA bus, playing in the back row. (Where, presumably, he heard "Loser" chants for an entirely different reason.) Granted, this wasn't the most promising start, but over the next few years, the L.A. scene began to grow—and so did Beck's ego, as hinted at in the Ben Folds song "Fired."

All eyes seemed to focus on the West Coast thanks to nerd-rockers **Weezer** gaining the admiration of Matt Pinfield and *Alternative Nation* viewers everywhere when songs like "Say It Ain't So" and "Buddy Holly" wooed thousands of wide-eyed fans who were years away from being creeped out by singer Rivers Cuomo's pervy fascination with Asian girls. However, while the members of Weezer were busy becoming emo gods, many of their peers in L.A. weren't even able to get arrested—like their pals in **That Dog**, who failed to reach a widespread audience despite the fact that the band featured a pair of hot twins, one of whom kind of looked like Sarah Jessica Parker,* and both of whom constantly wore miniskirts on-stage. Weezer bassist Matt Sharp later formed a side project called **the Rentals** with some of That Dog's members, in addition to *Saturday Night Live*'s Maya Rudolph. (Who knew?)

By the late '90s, both the Rentals and Weezer were starting to fizzle and both bands went on hiatus. At that point, the scene was starting to slow down, as well. In fact, at the time, the best-known local musician was quickly becoming **Elliott Smith**, an L.A. transplant who moved to La La Land after spending years in Portland, though he never quite assimilated, as proven by the fact that the guy constantly walked around wearing a beanie and hooded sweatshirt in ninety-degree heat. Always the outsider, Smith had very few peers in L.A. whom he could relate to. In fact, one of the only bands he frequently played with was **Beachwood Sparks**, a bunch of former hardcore kids who decided to reinvent themselves as a psychedelic hippie band and who preferred to walk around barefoot. Smith also bonded with L.A. upstarts **Rilo Kiley**, which had just finished recording its third album at his studio at the time of his untimely death. (The band even offered a tribute in the form of the *More Adventurous* closer "It Just Is.")

While Smith's death seemed to knock the scene on its knees, the city experienced a musical resurgence when a bunch of former child actors came down from their parents' mansions and began playing in tiny clubs on the east side of Hollywood. The most notable among these new groups were, of course, Rilo Kiley (which included the Girl from *Troop Beverly Hills* on vocals and the Dude from *Salute Your Shorts* on guitar), and **Phantom Planet** (which included the Dude from *Rushmore* on drums and the Dude from *Donnie Darko* on lead vocals). Now, as refreshing as it was to see Jenny Lewis and Jason Schwartzman get some props for having legitimate musical talent,

---

* Back in the '90s, this was considered a good thing. After all, this was *after* SJP earned major cred by dating Robert Downey, Jr., and *before* she started to morph into a horse.

there was one major problem: They also hung out with some major douchebags like, oh, anyone from **Maroon 5**. Formerly known as Kara's Flowers, M5 played their earliest shows with Rilo Kiley and Phantom Planet far before people realized that singer Adam Levine was one of the most unlikable dudes walking the face of the earth. (Seriously, that guy is the worst. Not only did he allegedly hook up with Jessica Simpson while she was still married, but when they broke up, he supposedly dumped her via text message. Damn, that's cold. So cold that he actually made me feel bad for her, which is really, *really* hard to do.)

It's no wonder then that the L.A. scene today has become a parody of what once was. It's more about scoring a headline on TMZ or face time in the pages *Us Weekly* than playing *good* music. However, there is still a small group of bands that are trying to take a trip in the way-back machine to a time when L.A. was all about down-and-dirty punk rock. *Period.* For that reason, shows often take place these days in more underground venues like the Smell, a sketchy warehouse space in downtown L.A. where you can usually catch experimental rock bands—and possibly tuberculosis. Although you take the risk of getting carjacked while trying to find a parking spot out front, you can also manage to see killer sets by groups like **No Age** and **Mika Miko**, which will inevitably be playing to a bunch of kids wearing loud, all-over-print Kidrobot hoodies. Now that's *my* idea of a good time.

HOW DO OTHER CELEBRITY BANDS MEASURE UP?

Like I mentioned in the section above, Los Angeles is a scene bursting with actors who want to be musicians (and vice versa). If you crunch the numbers, very few bands manage to get it right and earn the respect of the local music scene. So how does everyone in L.A. measure up? Let's take a look at the difference between the contenders who can read sheet music and the ones who are just reading cue cards.

DOGSTAR* SCALE OF EXCELLENCE

* = Musical equivalent of *Sweet November*. Big names but totally overrated.

** = Musical equivalent of *A Scanner Darkly*. Good in theory; bad in execution.

*** = Musical equivalent of *Bill and Ted's Excellent Adventure*. Middle America will love it but anyone with a keen ear will tear it to shreds.

**** = Musical equivalent of *The Matrix*. Stiff and somewhat unnatural, but completely and utterly entertaining.

***** = Musical equivalent of *Devil's Advocate*. So captivating and believable, you almost forget you're watching—and listening—to a bunch of actors.

30 SECONDS TO MARS * * *

THE DEAL: No one had high hopes for Jared Leto's musical career after seeing him front the fictional alt-rock band Frozen Embryos on the early '90s teenage drama *My So-Called Life*. However, once 30 Seconds to Mars scored a major-label deal with Virgin Records, launched an apocalyptic street team/fan club called the Echelon (which fans *actually* joined) and started touring with credible bands like the Used and My Chemical Romance, Leto & Co. became hard to ignore.

THE DIRT: Sure, Leto and his bandmates might have started off as nü-metal cronies, but it wasn't long until they hitched themselves to the emo bandwagon. After the release of their second album, *A Beautiful Lie*, they wisely began ripping off their new tourmates' sound—and smoky-eye application techniques—and it worked. The album

---

* Dogstar was the band that Keanu Reeves formed in the early '90s shortly after starring in the cinematic masterpiece *Point Break*, which has since become a traveling musical you can see in clubs across the country. For many scene purists, the band's brand of iffy alt-rock became the bar against which other musical vanity projects were judged. In other words, Dogstar is largely responsible for why most music fans think actor-bands suck.

sold like gangbusters and earned the group slots on legitimate tours (with bands like Head Automatica and Reggie and the Full Effect) and festivals (like the Bamboozle Left and Give It a Name). If it weren't for the fact that Leto insists on wearing silver Crocs and has an ego the size of China, we could totally get behind the band. Until then, we'll hum along with "The Kill"—but continue to tell anyone who listens that he supposedly has a collection of girls' private parts on his cell phone. F'reals.

JULIETTE AND THE LiCKS * *

THE DEAL: More than a decade after starring in such films as *Cape Fear* and *Natural Born Killers*, Juliette Lewis started a Stooges tribute band called the Licks with a couple of veteran musicians from the L.A. rock scene. Wait, what's that? The Licks weren't *actually* a Stooges tribute band? So she was dressing like that on purpose? Oops, my bad. She certainly sounded like a second-rate Iggy Pop on albums such as 2005's *Like a Bolt of Lightning*.

THE DIRT: While it's rather admirable that a talented actress like Lewis would do something as unglamorous as play a side stage on the Warped Tour (which the Licks did during the summer of 2004), let's get real: Iggy Pop can barely pull off Iggy Pop these days, let alone a thirtysomething, rail-thin actress who thrashes around stage in a lamé leotard, red kneepads, and an Indian headdress.

SHE AND HiM * * * * *

THE DEAL: Listeners got a taste of Zooey Deschanel's vocal styling in 2003's *Elf* and on the debut album of Coconut Records, *Nighttiming*, which just so happens to be the solo project of former Phantom Planet drummer and Deschanel ex-boyfriend Jason Schwartzman. However, it wasn't until hooking up with indie-folk artist M. Ward that Deschanel went from being yet another wide-eyed, wannabe singer to an indie-rock chanteuse and NPR darling.

THE DIRT: Over the last couple years, M. Ward has earned mucho respect for working with artists like Bright Eyes, Norah Jones, and Neko

<33>

Case. Combine his production skills with Deschanel's painstaking voice—which could stand up next to legendary country singers like Dusty Springfield or Patsy Cline—and I'm betting their debut album *Volume One* is only the beginning for She and Him. Plus, putting the record out on Merge is almost enough to earn her back the indie cred she lost when she decided to go blond. *Almost.*

WiCKED WiSDOM *

THE DEAL: Though they are often categorized as a heavy metal or hard-rock act, Wicked Wisdom is probably best described as pure comedy. C'mon, there's nothing funnier than for-mer *A Different World* star Jada Pinkett Smith sweat-ing profusely while sporting cornrows, a wife beater, and fronting a laughable rock band with dudes named Wirm, Rio, and Pocket Honore.

THE DIRT: Where's Ashton? I'm totally get-ting *Punk'd* with this shit, right? If not, then this might be the best-slash-worst thing I'm ever heard. If songs like "Bleed All Over Me" and "Reckoning" don't scare you, then take a look at Smith's demonic facial expressions and overdramatic hand movements while she's performing. Homegirl's got a bigger God complex than Scott Stapp. I wonder if Xenu and the rest of his Scientologist brethren would be stoked about that.

ROONEY * * * *

THE DEAL: If you obsessively watched the first season of *The O.C.,* then you already know that Rooney provided the soundtrack to the episode where Oliver, Marissa's crazy friend from rehab, goes nuts after listening to the band's sweet, Beach Boys–inspired songs. Shit got pretty scary for Ryan and the gang, but not as frightening as appearances from singer/guitarist Robert Carmine in *The Princess Diaries* and drummer Ned Brower on *Dawson's Creek*.

THE DIRT: Despite writing two albums worth of solid, sunny pop songs, Rooney is still largely known for being "that band on *The O.C.*" Unfortunately for them, it would seem that they're destined to suffer the same fate as Mischa Barton, who is also considered washed up at the tender age of twenty-one. (Coincidence or correlation, Barton was once romantically linked to Rooney guitarist Taylor Locke. Congratulations, lovebirds! I can't think of a more uninteresting couple.)

OH, SEE . . . WHY ORANGE COUNTY IS SO NOT L.A.

When hanging out in Los Angeles, do not, any under circumstance, suggest to a local scenester that you want to make a trip to Orange County. This will always end badly. Trust me. Yes, many of those same scenesters will drive an hour into the city only to step over a dead body in order to see some hot new band play at an illegal loft space Downtown, but bring up a trip to Orange County and it's like you just admitted to voting for McCain. So why do people dislike this place so much? Well, for one, Orange County is the kind of area where you can find tons of people who will openly admit they voted McCain without any of the requisite shame associated with such a decision. But that's hardly where it ends. I have two words for you: Lauren Conrad. In a nutshell, that pretty much summarizes why L.A. locals loathe the folks living behind the Orange Curtain. Still don't get it? I dare you to get through an entire episode of *The Hills* without being convinced that Conrad is actually the Antichrist. Go ahead. I double-dog dare you!

YOU ARE WHAT YOU LOVE

Every scene needs a muse and when it comes to Los Angeles, that source of stylistic inspiration comes from Rilo Kiley's Jenny Lewis.

Like Cher, Lewis has reinvented herself more times than I can remember; and, like Cher, she's also become an object of much affection for her male fans. You can tell a lot about a guy based on his love for Lewis. Allow me to translate what your level of obsession, er, adoration says about you.

ERA: CIRCA *TROOP BEVERLY HILLS* (COLUMBIA, 1989) AND *THE WIZARD* (UNIVERSAL, 1989)

WHAT SHE WAS LIKE: Armed with a killer side ponytail and stirrup leggings, Lewis made her cinematic mark alongside Hollywood heavy-hitters* like Shelley Long (in *Troop Beverly Hills*) and Fred Savage (in *The Wizard*) at the tender age of thirteen. Though she hinted at musical ambitions by singing backup vocals in *Troop*'s infamous "Cookie Time" scene, it would be another dozen years until Lewis would abandon acting completely to become the singer of an indie-rock band. Until then, she would spend most of her time filming movies destined for Lifetime television. (I recommend *Sweet Temptation*, a riveting drama about a rebellious sixteen-year-old girl who falls for her mother's boyfriend.)

WHAT THIS SAYS ABOUT YOU: If you loved this era of Lewis's career, then you're probably a total perv. Oh, and in case you were wondering, there's also a good chance you'll face a run-in with Chris Hansen† in the somewhat near future.

---

* At the time, Long and Savage were considered big box-office draws. These days, you can find Savage directing episodes of the dark comedy *It's Always Sunny in Philadelphia* and Disney's *Wizards of Waverly Place*. If you're looking for Long, check the waiting room of her plastic surgeon. Have you seen how tight that lady's face is lately? *Geez.*

† TV reporter and host of *Dateline*'s "To Catch a Predator," which is an ongoing news segment and series that baits potential online predators with bogus underage paramours. Who knew that catching potential pedophiles walking into a teen's house with a plastic bag filled with porn and lube would be *so* much fun to watch?

ERA: CIRCA *TAKE OFFS AND LANDINGS* (BARSUK, 2001) AND *THE EXECUTION OF ALL THINGS* (SADDLE CREEK, 2002)

WHAT SHE WAS LIKE: By this point, Lewis had cut her hair like Princess Zelda* and started Rilo Kiley with fellow former child star and boyfriend Blake Sennett. During this period, she also opted for cotton miniskirts, thrift-store tees, and the always fashion-forward trend of vintage dresses over jeans. I'm not sure what stylists Clinton Kelly and Stacy London from TLC's *What Not to Wear* would say about this look, but I'm pretty sure Lewis made looking like a bag lady work *waaay* before either of the Olsen twins did.

WHAT THIS SAYS ABOUT YOU: You recall the late '90s just a little *too* fondly. This also suggests that you may still live in your parents' basement, that you frequently listen to the first Apples in Stereo's record, and that any reference you make to "the woman in your life" is really just a fancy-pants way of talking about your mom.

ERA: CIRCA *MORE ADVENTUROUS* (BRUTE/BEAUTE, 2004)

WHAT SHE WAS LIKE: Although Lewis ended her relationship with Sennett before the release of Rilo Kiley's third album, that didn't exactly make the budding indie princess available to the average Rilo Kiley fan. Instead, Lewis spent the next few years allegedly getting down with Bright Eyes' Conor Oberst and Death Cab for Cutie's Ben Gibbard. She also began donning the kind of weird gypsy-esque dresses and frilly sashes that you could pick up at Stevie Nicks's next yard sale.

WHAT THIS SAYS ABOUT YOU: You really want a gypsy queen in your life, so much so that you won't shut up about how "life-altering" Fleetwood Mac's *Rumours* album was.

ERA: CIRCA *RABBIT FUR COAT* (TEAM LOVE, 2006)

WHAT SHE WAS LIKE: By the mid-2000s, Sennett decided to put out an album with his side project the Elected and Lewis also pursued

---

* This was a look that many female leaned toward in the late '90s that made them look like the Nintendo video game character as well as F. Scot.... Ugh, didn't you buy the last book? Do I really need to explain this *again*?

her own solo career with the release of her first country-tinged album *Rabbit Fur Coat*. Backed by the Watson Twins, Lewis paid musical homage to Dolly Parton, Emmylou Harris, and Loretta Lynn during this era. Stylistically, her look included the presence of hoop skirts, big hair, and large, inflatable boobs. Okay, maybe I'm wrong about the boobs, but she did look unusually busty on the album cover, don't you think?

WHAT THIS SAYS ABOUT YOU: You clearly like an older, more dignified woman with a shit-ton of childhood issues (and a C cup). That said, be prepared to throw down some major cash for your next girlfriend's therapy sessions—and frequent shopping trips to La Perla.

ERA: CIRCA *UNDER THE BLACKLIGHT* (WARNER BROS., 2007)

WHAT SHE WAS LIKE: When Lewis rekindled her musical romance with Rilo Kiley, she ditched the mini-dresses in favor of gold lamé marching-band uniforms. Some found this puzzling, but it didn't seem to bother current boyfriend Jonathan Rice, whose only claim to fame is the fact that he can be referred to as Lewis's "current boyfriend Jonathan Rice." It also didn't bother the droves of male fans who preferred to watch the Rilo Kiley frontwoman perform without any pants on.

WHAT THIS SAYS ABOUT YOU: You're the dude in the audience who has been lusting after her for ten years and who, moreover, is overjoyed by the fact that she's finally acknowledged your admiration by dressing like a pole dancer.

MAPPING OUT LOS ANGELES

AMERICAN APPAREL (2111 SUNSET BLVD., LOS ANGELES, CA 90026; HTTP://WWW.AMERICANAPPAREL.NET)

Surely, it won't be long until some apathetic hipster attempts to visit every American Apparel store in the country—much like that weirdo known only as "Winter" who made it his life's ambition to visit every Starbucks in the world—and when that person does, they'll start here at the first retail store ever opened by owner (and Tom Selleck look-alike) Dov Charney. Be careful, though. Before you throw some change to the long-haired, dingy-looking guy leaning in the doorway, there's a good chance he isn't really homeless. He's just Shwayze's Cisco Adler preparing to load up on deep V-neck T-shirts.

EAT WELL (3916 W SUNSET BLVD., LOS ANGELES, CA 90029)

If you are ever hung over on a Sunday morning (and, really, who in the Los Angeles music scene *isn't*), then this chain of diners is probably where you're going to soak up all the alcohol from the previous night's festivities. There are plenty of vegan options at Eat Well (like "The Big Mess," which is, as the name implies, a big mess of tofu and stuff), but more important, everything here comes with greasy, pan-fried potatoes. Oh, and if you are a real L.A. scenester, you'll definitely want to bow your head at the Eat Well in Silver Lake, where Death Cab for Cutie filmed part of its video for "The New Year."

AMOEBA MUSIC (6400 W SUNSET BLVD., LOS ANGELES, CA 90028; HTTP://WWW.AMOEBAMUSIC.COM)

Amoeba is like the Filene's Basement of CDs and vinyl—you're destined to find a unique treasure as long as you're patient. Touted as the "World's Largest Independent Music Store" and taking up an entire city block, Amoeba actually has three California locations (including

Berkeley and San Francisco), but the Hollywood store is really a sight to be seen. Whether you're waiting in line to see Vampire Weekend play an in-store or hoping you can finally get your hands on a copy of Heatmiser's *Mic City Sons* on vinyl, you should probably enter Amoeba in your GPS, like, *now.*

CINESPACE (6356 HOLLYWOOD BLVD., LOS ANGELES, CA 90028; HTTP://WWW.CINESPACE.INFO)

If you've bookmarked Cory Kennedy's blog on your Web browser, can name *any* member of the Like, and own the entire set of Cobrasnake limited-edition tees, then there's a good chance you're a regular at Cinespace—and your name is probably Steve Aoki. Yes, the crowd tends to be kind of douchey, but they're easy to ignore if you're there for Cinespace's signature dinner-and-a-movie events every Friday and Saturday night.

SOLUTIONS AUDIO (4334 SUNSET BLVD., LOS ANGELES, CA 90029)

As most residents of Echo Park already know, the Elliott Smith memorial is located on a brightly painted wall outside Solutions Audio, an old-school music supply shop that's been around since the late '60s. It was here that the late Elliott Smith stood in front of the store's red and navy swirled painting for the cover of his album *Figure 8*. After his death, fans initiated the wall as the site of his memorial and, over

<40>

the years, Sharpie-packing devotees from all over the world have visited this spot, leaving such heartfelt messages as "Portland misses you" and "I just met Drew Barrymore and I miss you very, very much!" Sadly, the wall seems to get repainted every couple months, so if you want your message to stand the test of time, you might have to visit frequently and reapply.

HIGH VOLTAGE TATTOO (1259 N LA BREA AVE., WEST HOLLYWOOD, CA 90038; HTTP://WWW.HIGHVOLTAGETATTOO.COM)

Owned and operated by famed human doodle pad Kat Von D, High Voltage is where all the inked magic happens on TLC's *L.A. Ink*. If you have ever come across the show (and, let's be real here, you probably have while cruising the channel for *What Not to Wear* reruns) then you have no doubt seen Von D and her crew tat up everyone from Sebastian Bach to members of Queens of the Stone Age. Walk-ins are welcome at High Voltage, just make sure you don't park in the Ralphs supermarket parking lot because your ass is sure to get towed.

<41>

THREE CLUBS COCKTAIL LOUNGE (1123 VINE ST., LOS ANGELES, CA 90038; HTTP://WWW.THREECLUBS.COM)

Since opening in the early 2000s, this L.A. dive bar has become a final destination for anyone who wants to experience the seedy underbelly of Hollywood without really getting all that dirty. Boasting live rock 'n' roll and plenty of DJ dance remixes, Three Clubs is also known for attracting the likes of hard-partying bands like the Bronx, Your Enemies Friends, and the Icarus Line. For the ten of you who still care about Courtney Love, it's also worth noting that L.A. trendsetter Cali DeWitt (the Artist Formerly Known as Francis Bean Cobain's nanny) tends bar here. This place is totally kid-tested; Courtney approved.

CHA CHA LOUNGE (2375 GLENDALE BLVD., LOS ANGELES, CA 90039; HTTP://WWW.CHACHALOUNGE.COM)

If you didn't go Greek during your college years (and, thus, didn't spend endless hours inside a tiki bar), this campy Silver Lake dive may be the place for you. You can easily tap into your inner frat boy or sorority sister in one of the Cha Cha's straw-covered booths or, better yet, get ridiculously drunk and begin making out with some underage hottie in the parking lot. That's the sort of role the Cha Cha currently occupies: It's sort of like L.A.'s answer to Señor Frog's, only no self-respecting customer would ever be caught dead here wearing a polo shirt from Hollister. A few miles away, however . . .

THE SHORT STOP (1455 W SUNSET BLVD., LOS ANGELES, CA 90026)

. . . you'll find the Short Stop, whose regulars have absolutely *no* problem with looking like the members of Kappa Sigma Toolbox. It wasn't always this way, though. Back in the day, when former Afghan Whigs frontman Greg Dulli converted this old cop bar into a hipster haven, you could regularly find Elliott Smith talking with the peeps from Rilo Kiley about what their favorite Byrds album is. These days? Not so much. Now local hipsters have to share bar space with the kind of people who would have given them swirlies in high school, and we all know how bad that sucks. Not like I've ever gotten a swirly or anything. Um . . . Quick, someone change the subject.

SPACELAND (1717 SILVER LAKE BLVD., LOS ANGELES, CA 90027; HTTP://WWW.CLUBSPACELAND.COM)

Traditionally, bands from L.A. want to get extremely famous very quickly and spend as little time playing in tiny clubs as possible. Oh, sure, everyone will *say* they love the kind of clubs that can barely accommodate the cast of *Little People, Big World*, but once your typical L.A. band gets a record deal, it's all about getting its grubby hands on a tour bus and having one of its songs featured on *The Hills*.

That said, when Spaceland opened in the mid-'90s, it seemed like just another club most local bands would forget about once they got to the top. So why does Spaceland still remain *the* club to play on the east side of Los Angeles? Simple: Because on the east side of Los Angeles, bands don't care about getting famous, as is illustrated by the caliber of bands booked at Spaceland. (Hell, it's not like on the Sunset Strip, where bands dream of being offered a record deal after causing a bar fight at the Viper Room.) Take a look at the venue's event calendar and you'll find a bunch of generic indie-rock bands with, well, incredibly generic indie-rock band names. (Delta Spirit and Sea Wolf, anyone?)

Anyone who doesn't love Spaceland for the club's lack of proactiveness is totally missing the point, because if the bands that routinely play here had grand ambitions, then this would be a *very* different club. As it stands, even the staff seems to be made up of slackers, as proven by the fact that the marquee out front still reads "Dreams," which was the name of the gay bar that used to occupy the space back in the late '80s.

WHITE TRASH CHARMS (1951 HILLHURST AVE., LOS ANGELES, CA 90027; HTTP://WWW.WHITETRASHCHARMS.COM)

No respectable L.A. scenester would be caught dead without at least one piece of iconic bling from White Trash Charms. Founded by celebrity stylist Brooke Dalien, WTC has been a jewelry fave for local bands like She Wants Revenge, Rooney, and theStart. Whether you're rocking their keyboard charm (like Kelly Osbourne) or their "Cute as a Button" charm (à la Hilary Duff), your neck would be naked without a White Trash charm.

THE SILVERLAKE LOUNGE (2906 SUNSET BLVD., LOS ANGELES, CA 90026; HTTP://WWW.FOLDSILVERLAKE.COM)

In many ways, the Silverlake Lounge feels like Spaceland's little brother. It doesn't get the same amount of respect as the Land and, astonishingly, it has even less space, but all sorts of local bands are bound to turn up here. In fact, Silversun Pickups named themselves after the liquor store that is located directly across the street (Silversun Liquor). I even heard that a common preshow tradition for the band was watching its rail-thin singer Brian Aubert get hit on by the fortysomething gay guys who were always hanging out at the coffee shop next door. (Note: If you are a rail-thin singer who also plans on playing here someday, consider yourself warned.)

A MOMENT OF SILENCE

JABBERJAW (3711 W PICO BLVD., LOS ANGELES, CA 90019)

When the Jabberjaw opened in the early '90s, it was a great time in L.A. for bands that played power chords and preferred not to wash their hair for weeks at a time. So it's no wonder that the club became famous for hosting surprise sets by then-hugely popular alt-rock bands like Nirvana and Everclear. At the time, however, what really set the 'Jaw apart was its location. You see, the Jabberjaw was located in Compton. (You know Compton, right? Ice Cube used to rap about it, John Singleton used to make terrifying movies about it, and, for some reason, lots of people seemed to shoot at each other there.) Needless to say, the Jabberjaw's locale was *rough* and surviving a night in the hood certainly gave local scenesters something to talk about.

Oftentimes, it wouldn't be unusual to overhear conversations that went a little something like this: "Hey man. Remember that time we

LOS ANGELES, CALIFORNIA

went to see Unwound play at the Jabberjaw and someone stole their van while they were loading in?" or "Do you remember the time Fitz of Depression played and Drew Barrymore and Courtney Love showed up drunk on Robitussin?" Crazybrains, right? When you think about it, that says a lot about how unique this club *actually* was. Despite the fact that you ran the risk of getting shot in a drive-by, L.A. music fans still showed up here in droves—that is, until the club finally closed down in the late '90s. The Make-Up was the last band to take the stage, and in typical Jabberjaw fashion, the band's performance was interrupted by a police helicopter swarming overhead. Then, as everyone filed outside, a homeless person began yelling at the club's owners. (I couldn't make this shit up if I tried.) Within weeks after its closing, the club transformed into a run-of-the-mill hardware store. If you make sure to lock your car doors, you can still go down and pay your respects. When you find yourself surrounded by an inordinate number of stores selling hair extensions, you know you're getting close.

September 30, 1997

A small, Ohio-based label named Doghouse Records releases Four Minute Mile, *the debut LP from a small Kansas City, Missouri–based band named the Get Up Kids. Misunderstood teen-agers all over the Midwest now have a new batch of musical heroes who totally "get them"—despite being in their early to mid-twenties.*

Lawrence, Kansas

Though most consider Kansas to be as wholesome as apple pie, the Lawrence music scene is inexplicably riddled with college dropouts and angst-ridden suburbanites who would rather smoke some grass than husk some corn. Oh, yeah, it's also home to some of the most influential second-wave emo bands of all time.

MUSIC PRIMER

All you newbies out there are probably wondering where to start when it comes to filling your Last.fm profile with Lawrence-based bands. Lucky for you, pretty much everyone that matters agrees that the scene started back in the early '90s when bands like **Boys Life** and **Giant's Chair** began to shape what was then known as "second-wave emo." "Hold up, Leslie," you cry. "Did I miss the first wave of emo? Whatchu talkin' 'bout, Willis?" Easy, Gary Coleman. The first wave of emo went down in Washington D.C. with bands like Rites of Spring and Embrace.[*] It was Lawrence and other neighboring Midwestern towns, however, that became ground zero for emo's second wave, which was a precursor to the sound a lot of guys in eyeliner would make millions of dollars off of two decades later.

Boys Life and Giant's Chair tapped into their Midwestern roots and love of post-hardcore to inspire other bands in the scene to write

[*] Don't get your undies in a twist, dear reader. Just refer back to page 3 for a refresher course.

sentimental songs about such diverse topics as fire trucks and geography. It wouldn't be long before they were joined by a bunch of kindred spirits from nearby Topeka called **Vitreous Humor**, which was led by a geeky and gawky frontman named Danny Pound. The band had tons in common with the overtly emotional dudes in Boys Life, and to prove it, they released a split EP together that included the Vitreous fan favorite "Why Are You So Mean to Me?" which might just be the most emo song title *ever*.

While bands like Vitreous Humour and Boys Life tried *not* to get beat up by keeping things sappy, another group of locals called **Coalesce** proved that Kansas wasn't only populated by wussy dudes in V-neck sweaters who played sad love songs. Instead, Coalesce was a group of wussy-looking dudes in V-neck T-shirts who played extremely loud and aggressive hardcore music. Their shows were legendary in Lawrence, and to this day, it's still not all that uncommon to overhear conversations that begin with, "Hey, were you at the Coalesce show where the guitarist started masturbating?" or "Hey, weren't you at that basement show in Eudora where the singer from Coalesce choke-slammed some dude's little brother while the rest of the band painted pentagrams on each other's naked bodies in red paint?"

Okay, that last thing didn't really happen, but as anyone who was living in Lawrence at the time will tell you, it definitely could have. In fact, one band that can personally attest to this was **the Get Up Kids**, a melodic emo band that played an infamous show with Coalesce in the mid-'90s at which the latter band's drummer, James Dewees, threw a floor tom at some girl's head. Coincidence or correlation, Dewees was asked to play keyboards in the Get Up Kids just a few months later and became a full-fledged member of the group upon the release of the band's 1999 Vagrant Records debut, *Something to Write Home About*. It was during this era that the band quickly graduated from performing in grimy basements with Dewees to riding around in a tour bus and playing sold-out concerts.

For some reason, that last part caused a huge amount of resentment from the locals in Lawrence and many scenesters started to criticize the band for mobilizing fans through this relatively new invention called "the Internet." Talking seemed like a waste of time, though, seeing that the attention surrounding the Get Up Kids and the rest of the Lawrence scene had only begun. In the coming months, Los Angeles's **the Appleseed Cast** decided to give up seventy-degree weather in order to move to Lawrence, and while it never did quite make it to the big time, up-and-coming local bands like **the Anniversary** came pretty close, after signing to the same label as the Get Up Kids and releasing its Moog-tastic debut, *Designing a Nervous Breakdown*.

Of course, the Anniversary owed a lot of its initial success to the fact that its keyboardist Adrianne Verhoeven was married to the Get Up Kids' bassist Rob Pope at the time. But they were hardly alone in their wedded bliss, because by the early 2000s, pretty much everyone in Lawrence was married. This *is* the Midwest, after all. What else is there to do? That said, it was inevitable that coupledom would start to affect the music—for better (like any **New Amsterdams** albums, which are inevitably inspired by the domestic life of family man Matt Pryor) or for worse (like the **Reggie and the Full Effect** album called *Songs Not To Get Married To*, which chronicles Dewees's tumultuous divorce).

What I mean is that both the Get Up Kids and the Anniversary did what most musicians do when they attempt to settle down: They started ripping off classic-rock bands. The Get Up Kids decided to go with the Beatles, as heard on their 2002 album *On a Wire*. The Anniversary, on the other hand, decided to swipe the sound—and the look—of vintage Fleetwood Mac when putting out its sophomore album, *Your Majesty*. In what seemed like the blink of an eye, the band's members traded their tight ringer tees and knit beanies for corduroy loon pants and denim vests, leading many to believe they had completely lost their minds. But that was the least of their worries. By early 2003, the Verhoeven-Pope union was over and, in turn, so was the Anniversary's contract with Vagrant Records, the indie label it shared

with Pope's band. Rumors circulated throughout the scene that infidelity was to blame for the split, but the couple refused to confirm or deny. (If you're a nosey parker and thrive on drama, take a listen to "Never Be Alone" off the Get Up Kids' 2004 album *Guilt Show* and you'll pretty much have your answer.)

Now, while it's not completely fair to say that the Lawrence scene fell apart in the years that followed, you could definitely argue that a lot changed from that point on. Both the Anniversary and the Get Up Kids broke up shortly thereafter, which inspired the Get Up Kids' frontman to form a *side* side project, **the Terrible Twos**. Instead of writing about drinking cheap whiskey (as with the New Amsterdams), Pryor scribbled songs about mischievous little brothers ("Big Baby J"), broccoli ("When I Get to Eleven"), and toddlers who have really poor hygiene ("Archibald McCallister"). Pryor even went so far as to perform in local elementary schools, which is pretty weird—but not half as weird as what the Anniversary's Justin Roelofs did after his band came to an end. You see, not only did he begin performing psychedelic-tinged indie-rock under the name **White Flight**, but he also grew his hair out, wore schmatas, started to look eerily similar to Jesus, and moved into a tepee out in the woods. (This last part is only speculation, but where else would homeboy be able to smoke his homegrown peyote? Again, more speculation, but this is *my* book and I'll speculate if I want to.) As for his former bandmates, the majority of them formed a new band called **the Only Children**, who did little to hide their love for beards and bell-bottoms, picking up where the music left off on *Your Majesty*.

Of course, the local scene in Lawrence has continued on with other new bands *not* associated with the Get Up Kids, like **Vedera**, a female-fronted rock band that many in town have referred to as the indie version of Evanescence—except that, unlike Evanescence, they actually write decent music. Then there's **Ad Astra Per Aspera**, an experimental noise-rock band that sounds like a listenable version of Sonic Youth. Don't forget about **Josephine Collective**, which has some of the tightest power-pop melodies this side of the Rocky Mountains, and **the Republic Tigers**, who scored major headlines when they became the first band signed to Alex Patsavas's Chop Shop Records. (Patsavas is only *the* greatest music supervisor of all time, having picked soundtracks for *The O.C.* and *Gossip Girl*. Yeah, *kind of* a big deal, right?) Sure, it's pretty awesome to be on Blair Waldorf's playlist, but for bands who boast about their Kansas pride, there truly is no place like home.

ESSENTIAL LAWRENCE, KANSAS, ALBUM GUIDE

Now that you've acquainted yourself with the city's musical history, it's easy to see how the scene has churned out dozens of essential albums by the best and brightest local bands. But who has the time to download and memorize them all? Once again, allow me to save you the effort by outlining all the essential releases you should have in your music library.

BOYS LIFE: *BOYS LIFE* (CRANK!, 1995)

WHAT YOU NEED TO KNOW: Before Mark Trombino made a name for himself producing albums by Jimmy Eat World and Blink-182, he hooked up with this band of Kansas City gents to record this dissonant and noisy post-hardcore masterpiece. With simple bass lines offset by mangled guitars and haywire vocals, the songs on *Boys Life* would help set the standard for the future of second-wave emo.

WHAT MAKES IT ESSENTIAL: The band called it quits soon after the release of their second full-length album, *Departures and Landfalls*, and members soldiered on in groups like the Farewell Bend and Canyon—none of which influenced future generations of guyliner enthusiasts as much as Boys Life.

THE GET UP KIDS: *FOUR MINUTE MILE* (DOGHOUSE, 1997)

WHAT YOU NEED TO KNOW: Recorded over two days in a Chicago studio with producer Bob Weston (Mission of Burma, Shiner), *Four Minute Mile* is a testament to the fact that big budgets and infinite studio time aren't required to make a groundbreaking album. (Hear that, Axl?) Instead, the Get Up Kids (pre–James Dewees) hit their stride with rough-around-the-edges emo anthems like "Don't Hate Me" and "Coming Clean," both of which remained set staples until the band called it quits in 2005.

WHAT MAKES IT ESSENTIAL: For critics and fans alike, *Four Minute Mile* is considered the blueprint for hook-laden, heartbreak-inspired Midwestern emo. While the Get Up Kids would embrace different musical styles over the years (Moog-rock with 1999's *Something to Write Home About* and indie-infused Americana with 2002's *On a Wire*), their Doghouse debut remains a must for those who call themselves a fan of emo—or music in general.

COALESCE: *GIVE THEM ROPE* (EDISON, 1997)

WHAT YOU NEED TO KNOW: Before tickling the ivories with the Get Up Kids (as well as New Found Glory and My Chemical Romance), James Dewees actually logged thousands of road miles as drummer and resident wildman of the Kansas City quartet Coalesce. *Give Them Rope* marked the band's full-length debut and is filled with the kind of terror, mayhem, and madness not often heard outside Sweden—or a rowdy village lockup. Warning: With songs like "One on the Ground" and "Have Patience," this album may cause brain damage, so prepare accordingly.

WHAT MAKES IT ESSENTIAL: Despite looking more like a bunch of schlubby extras from the 1995 movie *Kids* than a group of musical pioneers, Coalesce managed to define the burgeoning metal/hardcore genre with *Give Them Rope*. Although Dewees would go on to be a wingman in other bands (as mentioned above), the members of

Coalesce would spend the next years breaking up and reforming. Last I heard, a new album was in the works. Also, last I heard, not a lot of people seemed to care. Go figure.

VITREOUS HUMOR: *POSTHUMOUS* (CRANK!, 1998)

WHAT YOU NEED TO KNOW: After nearly ten years together, Vitreous Humor released what would be its last—and best—album, the ironically titled *Posthumous,*˙ which was filled with angular post-punk songs like "My Midget" and "Why Are You So Mean to Me?"

WHAT MAKES IT ESSENTIAL: *Posthumous* also included a song called "The Regrets," which was the name of the band singer Danny Pound, guitarist Brad Allen, and drummer Dan Benson formed just before Vitreous Humor split in 1998. Sure, the band never became much of a draw outside the Midwest, but old-school scenesters in Lawrence credit Pound and his posse with inspiring a generation of bands influenced by disjointed chords and distortion.

THE ANNIVERSARY: *DESIGNING A NERVOUS BREAKDOWN* (HEROES & VILLAINS, 2000)

WHAT YOU NEED TO KNOW: The Anniversary perfected the art of Moog-rock on its Vagrant debut and it wasn't long before songs like "The Heart Is a Lonely Hunter" and "Hart Crane" became instant classics among fans who liked their emo with a side of English literature. Although the band never broke through the mainstream with the single "All Things Ordinary," they certainly came close—*sort of.* Legend has it that after an intern at *TRL* showed Fred Durst the clip, the Limp Bizkit frontman (and Hair Club for Men member) stole the Lawrence quintet's video concept for his band's track "My Way." Calls to Durst weren't returned due to his busy schedule applying minoxidil. However, view the videos side-by-side on YouTube and judge for yourself!

WHAT MAKES IT ESSENTIAL: It's no dirty little secret that bands like the All-American Rejects and Hellogoodbye wouldn't be where they are today if not for the Moog-tastic emo on *Designing a Ner-*

---

* *adj.* Occurring after someone or something dies.

<55>

vous Breakdown. The Anniversary was definitely ahead of its time and inarguably burned out too fast, but its legacy lives on every time Motion City Soundtrack's Jesse Johnson does a scissor kick on his keyboard.

REGGIE AND THE FULL EFFECT: *PROMOTIONAL COPY* (VAGRANT, 2001)

WHAT YOU NEED TO KNOW: Depending on whom you believe, Reggie and the Full Effect is either the work of an agoraphobic bluesman or the side project of the Get Up Kids' James Dewees. Think what you will, not since Sally Field's performance in *Sybil* have I seen someone take on so many different personalities all in the name of art. In addition to drunken skits and Moog-infused Reggie hits, there are songs by Fluxuation, a newwave Brit-pop singer who is obsessed with spelling, and don't forget Common Denominator, a Finnish metal band that pays homage to little people on "Dwarf Invasion."

WHAT MAKES IT ESSENTIAL: Behind all the skits and shticks, *Promotional Copy* proves that Reggie and the Full Effect is a pitch-perfect emo-pop band—no matter how many different personalities and antipsychotic medications are involved. For those who missed him the first time around, back when Reggie (and Dewees) originally toured in support of this album, it was normal to witness a stage show featuring buckets of fake blood, electric fire engines, and Gerard Way dressed up in a giant bear suit. Ah, the good ol' days.

LAWRENCE, KANSAS

<56>

ULTIMATE FAKEBOOK: *OPEN UP AND SAY AWESOME* (INITIAL, 2002)

WHAT YOU NEED TO KNOW: Poor Ultimate Fakebook. In the early 2000s, the trio was the consummate opening act for fellow Lawrence groups like the Get Up Kids and Reggie and the Full Effect. Then Sony dropped them after their major-label debut *This Will Be Laughing Week* failed to meet expectations.* However, things started to look up when the power-pop trio released its 2002 album *Open Up and Say Awesome*, a collection of sugary-sweet, self-affirming pop songs like "When I'm With You, I'm OK" and "Before You Leave."

WHAT MAKES IT ESSENTIAL: Although many laughed the band off as Weezer wannabes, when Ultimate Fakebook broke up in 2004, it joined the likes of Third Eye Blind and Eve 6 as an unexpected inspiration to the next-generation of indie-pop bands. Down but not out, the members of Ultimate Fakebook are still in the biz: Bassist Nick Colby and drummer Eric Melin play together in the Dead Girls; Melin and former guitarist/singer J. D. Warnock run the movie news site Scene-Stealers.com; and former guitarist/singer Bill McShane is now a film editor and has worked on videos for Blackpool Lights and the Spill Canvas.

THE NEW AMSTERDAMS: *WORSE FOR THE WEAR* (VAGRANT, 2003)

WHAT YOU NEED TO KNOW: Thanks in part to the success of songs like "Hanging on for Hope" and "The Spoils of the Spoiled," which landed the band a coveted appearance on *The Late Show with David Letterman*, the New Amsterdams (featuring the Get Up Kids' frontman Matt Pryor) really broke out from side-project Siberia with the release of *Worse for the Wear*.

WHAT MAKES IT ESSENTIAL: Dashboard Confessional isn't the only band on Vagrant that features a thirtysomething family man singing pretty acoustic ballads about fleeting fame and lost youth. This album is the reason why.

---

* Translation: Shit bombed.

<57>

ON BENDED KNEE

Chock it up to wide-eyed optimism or good ol' traditional Midwestern values, but it seems as if everyone in Kansas decides to get married the day after they graduate high school. Though whether said scenesters stay married is a whole other topic altogether. According to Divorce Rate.org, almost 40 percent of all marriages end in divorce, with the highest rate of dissolution happening when the couple is under the age of twenty. Thems some shitty odds, huh? So why bother getting married? Here are a couple ideas . . .

TO BE AN ADULT

Some kids are just born to be adults—and I'm not talking about the ones suffering from progeria.* I mean those who, at an early age, start obsessing about the things most people don't sweat over until their mid-thirties. For example, you'll often find such toddlers asking questions like, "Mommy, when can I get a Roth IRA?" "Daddy, how much is the interest rate on our mortgage?" and "Nana, why do people still go see Woody Allen movies when he hasn't made a good one since *Annie Hall*?" It's this race to adulthood that causes many Midwestern teens to walk down the aisle before they're old enough to rent a hotel room. Luckily for them, nothing says "I'm a grown-up" like having your parents chaperone your honeymoon.

TO AVOID BEING ALONE

There's nothing more daunting than the potential of becoming an old maid who lives amongst a menagerie of cats and whose idea of a "good time" is attempt-

---

* *n.* Rare condition found in children that greatly accelerates the aging process. Few patients live past the age of thirteen. I'd like to write something snarky but I'm worried about going to hell.

<58>

ing to solve the mysteries alongside Angela Lansbury on *Murder She Wrote*. That said, it's no wonder Midwesterners have a tendency to say yes to the first person who buys them a Coney Cheese Dog at the A&W. Why wait for Mr. Right when Mr. Right Now is ready to give it a go?

TO MAKE YOUR RELATIONSHIP SECURE

Nothing fixes a potentially broken relationship better than getting hitched, right? Wrong—unless you're from the Midwest, where they believe that there isn't a doomed relationship that a three-carat diamond ring can't cure.

TO COMPENSATE FOR AN "ACCIDENT"

Sure, *Juno* made teenage pregnancy look like no big whoop, but in reality, I doubt any teenage girl would be *that* calm and collected to find out her Tic Tac–popping, non-boyfriend accidentally slipped one past the goalie. In fact, I've seen enough episodes of *Jerry Springer* to know that kids having kids is one of the fastest ways to ruin your otherwise carefree young adult life—well, that and finding out that the guy who impregnated you is actually your brother. (Man, that was a bitchin' episode.) Sure, accidents happen (though hopefully they *don't* happen with a blood relative), but that's why God invented wedding gowns with empire waists.

MAPPING OUT LAWRENCE

BLACK LODGE RECORDING (701 MAIN ST., EUDORA, KS 66025; HTTP://WWW.BLACKLODGERECORDING.COM)

Along with members of the Get Up Kids, producer Ed Rose opened up this top-of-the-line studio back in 2003. Over the years, bands like the Appleseed Cast, Motion City Soundtrack, Coalesce, Limbeck, and Reggie and the Full Effect have all recorded here. In addition to booking studio time, Rose also offers small-group recording workshops where wannabe producers can get behind the boards and gain some hands-on production experience. Want to learn the difference between dynamic processing and time-base processing? Yeah, me neither. But for the kind of music geeks living in Lawrence who keep their old issues of *Tape Op* in plastic slip covers, this place is a godsend.

THE BOTTLENECK (737 NEW HAMPSHIRE ST., LAWRENCE, KS 66044; HTTP://WWW.THEBOTTLENECKLIVE.COM)

Over the past twenty years, the Bottleneck—named after the huge beer selection sold here—has become *the* place to see live music in Lawrence. In addition to attracting local bands like the New Amsterdams and Blackpool Lights, the venue has also hosted shows from Radiohead, Foo Fighters, and Built to Spill. However, what distinguishes the Bottleneck as more than just a meager rock club is its locale (around the corner from the Replay Lounge and the rest of the strip on Massachusetts Street) and the other activities the venue offers.

For example, always one to exert hometown pride, the club holds open-mic nights every Monday where budding musicians can test their chops—and their ability to dodge a flying beer bottle, if they really suck. Then there's the Neon Dance Party, which happens every Thursday night with DJs Koncept or Cruz on the decks. These dudes might not know how to spell, but they are totally adept at spinning dance hits from the '80s and '90s. Finally, double your fun every Sunday when the bar hosts a rousing game of Smackdown! Trivia *and* free karaoke. Finally, all those lonely nights of playing *SingStar* are going to pay off!

HAMMERPRESS (110 SOUTHWEST BLVD., KANSAS CITY, MO 64108; HTTP://WWW.HAMMERPRESS.NET)

If you've ever been to a show in the greater Kansas City area, then you've probably seen a Hammerpress concert poster—and stolen it off the wall in order to adorn your bedroom. Known for layered-looking prints with bright colors and mismatching text, Hammerpress was started in 1994 by printmaker Brady Vest, who, over the past fifteen years, has helped create the visual aesthetic of Kansas's indie music scene (with the help of codesigner Lindsay Laricks), and introduced letterpress to a new generation of graphic artists.

KIEF'S DOWNTOWN MUSIC (823 MASSACHUSETTS ST., LAWRENCE, KS 66044; HTTP://WWW.DOWNTOWN.KIEFS .COM)

What started in 1959 as a simple music shop has now expanded into a bona fide superstore with two locations—in uptown and downtown Lawrence—that are both part of the illustrious Coalition of Independent Music Stores (CIMS). (Take that, Best Buy!) Not only will bohemian-looking, non-elitist salespeople cater to all your indie needs here, but Downtown's website is even updated regularly (what a concept!) with sales, staff picks, and tip sheets for new releases.

LIBERTY HALL (644 MASSACHUSETTS ST., LAWRENCE, KS 66045; HTTP://WWW.LIBERTYHALL.NET)

Besides Liberty Hall, we can't think of another American establishment that can brag about being around for 142 years. (Well, *maybe* Larry King.) The venue has been used for a variety of things over the past century and a half; in addition to being an opera house, music hall, meetinghouse, and video store, Liberty Hall also screens the latest and greatest independent films, which is a rarity in Lawrence.

LOCAL BURGER (714 VERMONT ST., LAWRENCE, KS 66044; HTTP://WWW.LOCALBURGER.COM)

Named by *Bon Appétit* magazine as one of America's Top Ten Eco-Friendly Restaurants, Local Burger is all about truth in advertising: You'll always know what you're eating (i.e., the grass-fed-only Elk Burger) and where it came from (i.e., Rocky Hills Elk Ranch in Winchester, Kansas), because this joint only serves locally grown organic food. *Period.* Sorry, folks. No mystery meat here!

<61>

LOVE GARDEN SOUNDS (936 1/2 MASSACHUSETTS ST., LAWRENCE, KS 66044; HTTP://WWW.LOVEGARDENSOUNDS .COM)

What would a college town be without a trusty used record store? For the residents of Lawrence, that's where Love Garden Sounds comes in. Co-owned and operated by Kory Willis, his wife Katie Conrad, and Kelly Corcoran (husband of local *All Things Considered* host Laura Lorson, for all you NPR lovers out there), Love Garden offers up an impressive selection of new and used CDs, hard-to-find vinyl, live band performances, and a try-it-before-you-buy-it policy.

However, what really sets Love Garden apart from the pack are the store's feline fixtures. Yup, a bunch of tabbies call the shop home and are known to attract customers just as much as a copy of the Ad Astra Per Aspera *Danger Bird Blues* 7-inch. Allergies aside, patrons seem to love the kitty companions. In fact, when Willis's fourteen-year-old cat Cayenne passed away in 2005, the whole community mourned and paid its respects. And here I thought hipsters only cared about wearing secondhand leather jackets and looking bored.

THE RECORD BAR (1020 WESTPORT RD., KANSAS CITY, MO 64111; HTTP://WWW.THERECORDBAR.COM)

The kitchen's open every night until 1:30 a.m. at the Record Bar, serving up music-inspired plates like I Melt with You (a hot turkey sandwich with sautéed spinach, caramelized onions, and Dijon mustard), the Birth of Cool (cold penne pasta tossed in a tomato vinaigrette), and Gangsta Wraps (made to order). Plus, while you're munching down on some savory treats, you can also check out some of the city's best up-and-coming acts like Ghosty and the Life and Times.

THE REPLAY LOUNGE (946 MASSACHUSETTS ST., LAWRENCE, KS 66044; HTTP://WWW.REPLAYLOUNGE.COM)

Boasting "the cleanest bathrooms in town," which isn't saying much, the Replay Lounge is perhaps most famous for the year-round, kick-ass beer garden and patio, which hosts local DJs, dance parties, and two-dollar cans of Pabst Blue Ribbon. As if you needed another reason to love the place, the Lounge is all about taking care of their own: When door guy Seth got jumped outside the venue, Lounge lizards rallied and threw the poor dude a benefit show (appropriately called "Benefit for Seth's Face") to cover his medical expenses.

A MOMENT OF SILENCE

THE OUTHOUSE (1837 N 1500 RD., LAWRENCE, KS 66046)

Though the name elicits visions of a pee and poop factory, the Outhouse was in fact *the* place to see punk rock in Lawrence during the 1980s. Located three miles east of Massachusetts Street, the Outhouse was really no more than a rundown shack surrounded by a muddy, unpaved parking lot, but to local scenesters, it was so much more than that: It was a place to escape from their parents, suburbia, and the wholesome Midwestern values that usually left them in shackles. Here, they could indulge in musical debauchery from bands like Naked Raygun, Descendents, and 7 Seconds, and partake in such hell-raising activities as painting a pig's head with tempera paint.

Unfortunately, as the '80s came to an end, so did the carefree vibe at the Outhouse. Skinheads started taking over the venue and with them came violent outbursts and the threat of physical harm to locals who just wanted to skank in peace. For fear of incident, shows were booked less and less, and it wasn't long until new clubs like the Replay Lounge swooped in to fill the punk-rock void. In 1998, the Outhouse flushed away any hope for a punk-rock resurgence when the new owner decided to use the building to fill another void left in the Lawrence scene: a BYOB, fully nude strip club.

Summer 1998

The seventh season of The Real World *airs on MTV. Although local residents are disgusted and take to wearing T-shirts that read "Seattle says: The Real World sucks!" the network spends six months exploiting—er, filming in Coffee Town. The final result follows seven tone-deaf morons plopped in the middle of the local music scene (thanks to an internship at a modern rock radio station) to see if they sink or swim in Lake Washington. Needless to say, there is an immediate shortage of life vests in the city.*

Seattle, Washington

When you think of Seattle, chances are you envision all sorts of thirty-something intellectuals who went to progressive universities and can talk endlessly about Godard films. That's not exactly right. What you'll really find in Seattle are thirtysomething intellectuals who can talk about Godard films and who *also* play in some of the most renowned alt-rock bands around.

MUSIC PRIMER

In addition to being the source of caffeine culture (thanks, Starbucks) and the Pacific Northwest's capital of serial killer activity, Seattle is primarily known for being the birthplace of grunge. Ah, to be back in 1992 again: Kurt and Courtney were voted cutest couple by drug dealers everywhere; *Singles* captured the American dream for every unemployed slacker in an alt-rock band; and thanks to fishnet stockings, Doc Martens boots *finally* started to lose that whole Nazi image they acquired in WWII.

I could write a hundred pages alone on the birth and death of grunge in Seattle, but I'd rather not OD on flannel this early in the chapter. Instead, let's center in on the band I consider responsible for launching the post-grunge scene in Seattle: **Sunny Day Real Estate**. Although the group originally started in 1992 as a trio playing hardcore music, soon thereafter, when guitarist Jeremy Enigk joined, the

band evolved its hardcore sound into what would be considered by many the first notes of emo. Their breakout album *Diary* contained songs (like "In Circles" and "Seven") that would eventually inspire future members of Saves the Day and Thursday to pick up guitars and start a band, but inner turmoil within Sunny Day (which was sparked by Enigk's sudden conversion to Christianity) led to the band's breakup in 1995. The original members would reunite two years later and even release two more albums (both of which fans weren't so stoked about), only to call it quits again in 2000—and this time it was for good.

Thankfully, the Seattle scene didn't mourn their loss for too long because bands like **Modest Mouse** and **Death Cab for Cutie** were coming up the ranks as two of the city's great indie hopes. Led by Isaac Brock and Ben Gibbard, respectively, both bands started up in the mid-'90s and wowed audiences with their electric live shows, indie-label outlooks (MM released albums on Up Records, DCFC on Barsuk), and DIY work ethics. It was Modest Mouse's 1997 album *The Lonesome Crowded West*, defined by disjointed and jangly rockers like "Trailer Trash" and "Polar Opposites," that really solidified the band as an indie force to reckon with—and an inexplicable guilty pleasure for jam-band fans* who liked to twirl around in circles for hours at a time. On the other hand, for those who yearned for music with a bit more melody (and concerts that didn't stink like body odor and patchouli), Death Cab for Cutie aimed to please with bitter rants like "For What Reason" (off 2000's *We Have the Facts and We're Voting Yes*) and lovesick vignettes like "A Movie Script Ending" (off 2001's *The Photo Album*).

Coincidentally, more than a decade later both bands would also receive mainstream recognition after releasing their major-label debuts—MM's *Good News for People Who Like Bad News* and DCFC's *Plans*—both of which redefined what it meant to be an "indie artist" and refocused mucho media attention back on Seattle. For those listening to KEXP 90.3,† however, the city's indie scene had never stopped thriving, thanks to **the Blood Brothers'** experimental post-hardcore, **Pretty Girls Make Graves's** art-punk aesthetic, **Trial's** straightedge hardcore, and **Botch's** defining brand of mathcore. Although all four of these groups would eventually disband, their members would remain active in the scene and start new groundbreaking bands like **Head Wound City** (featuring the Blood Brothers' Jordan Blilie and Cody Votolato), **Jaguar Love** (featuring the Blood Brothers' Votolato and Johnny Whitney, and Jay Clark from Pretty Girls Make Graves), **Minus the Bear** (featuring Botch's Dave Knudson), **These Arms Are Snakes** (featuring Botch's Brian Cook), and **Himsa** (featuring Trial's Derek Harn).

---

* For reasons unexplained by modern science, Modest Mouse remains one of the few bands that crossover to both hipsters *and* hippies, so don't be shocked if you see a group of unwashed, patchwork-wearing transients selling glass bowls and grilled cheeses in the parking lot before the next show. They're not bums; they're just jam-band fans who like a good, needling guitar solo as much as the next person. Plus, it's not like they have anything else to do until Phish gets back together.

† Seattle's premiere independent public radio station. You are not an official scenester unless you've got your car dial set to 90.3 FM and listen to its live stream on your computer at work.

SEATTLE, WASHINGTON

THE BATTLE IN SEATTLE
MON APR 9th *at the* **CROCODILE CAFE**

12 ROUNDS

BEN "MACHO" **GIBBARD** vs. ISAAC "TOUCH OF SLEEP" **BROCK**

While Seattle seemed to have hit its stride with indie bands, the scene continues to foster artists from a bevy of different genres: **This Providence** and **Amber Pacific** speak to the pop-punk population; **the Fall of Troy** is all about prog-rock; **Emery** attracts worshippers of Christian post-hardcore; and both **Aiden** and **Schoolyard Heroes** have blended horror punk with dramatic onstage theatrics. So what does Seattle sound like today? We'd have to say diverse.

LABEL CONSCIOUS

The greater Seattle metropolitan area is home to many different record labels like Barsuk and Suicide Squeeze, plus Kill Rock Stars and K Records, which reside in neighboring Olympia. However, if it weren't for

<71>

Sub Pop launching the infamous "Seattle sound" in the late '80s and Tooth & Nail carrying the post-hardcore torch at the turn of the new millennium, the scene as we know it today would cease to exist—and that's no good for anyone.

Originally named for the fanzine Bruce Pavitt published called *Subterranean Pop* (which was eventually shortened to simply "Sub Pop"), the label was officially launched in 1988 with the release of the compilation *Sub Pop 100*, which featured songs by non-Seattle-based bands like Sonic Youth, Naked Raygun, and Shonen Knife. Thankfully, a year later, Sub Pop released **Green River**'s *Dry as a Bone* EP, the first of many albums boasting a new "Seattle sound." Characterized by heavy metal and hardcore punk riffs, feedback effects, and obscene amounts of distortion, Sub Pop became ground zero for grunge after signing **Soundgarden**, **Mudhoney**, **Tad**, **Screaming Trees**, and, of course, this really unimportant band named **Nirvana**. (I jest.)

Sub Pop pretty much ruled the scene until the mid-'90s, when grunge turned into a punch line and outsiders like Best Buy and designer Alexander McQueen started using the trend as a way to sell Sony Walkmen and overpriced plaid quilts, respectively. Finally, when craptastic bands like Puddle of Mudd, Candlebox, and the Vines were all hailed as "the next Nirvana," Kurt Cobain could be heard bitching up a storm in heaven—like he really needs to deal with this crap after he's already pissed at someone for stealing his ashes—and Sub Pop entered into a rebirth period in which everyone cut their hair, stopped wearing flannel, and started tapping into then-underground talent like **Iron and Wine**, **the Thermals**, and **Hot Hot Heat**. However, it wasn't until the label released *Give Up* by **The Postal Service**—which started harmlessly enough as a side project between Death Cab for Cutie frontman Ben Gibbard and Dntel programmer Jimmy Tamborello—and the debut became the label's second bestselling album after Nirvana's *Bleach* that Pavitt & Co. reemerged as an independent music force to reckon with. Today, Sub Pop continues to put out groundbreaking albums by groups like indie-pop's **Band of Horses**, electro-pop's **CSS**, and the label's first Grammy Award–winning artists (if you can call two blubbering Kiwi comedians "artists"), **Flight of the Conchords**.

On the other side of the dial, **Tooth & Nail Records**, best known for bringing their roster of primarily Christian punk, metalcore, and screamo bands to the Hot Topic masses, was also recently recognized with a Grammy nod, but it was for Best Recording Package*—and they didn't win. Started in 1993 by a kid named Brandon Ebel who was inspired by the success of God-loving hardcore bands like the Crucified, Tooth & Nail has spent the past fifteen years pondering the eternal question: What would Jesus do? Well, if he were here today, he'd probably be rocking albums by **the Juliana Theory**, **MxPx**, and **Zao** to get all pumped up before he fulfilled his Messianic prophecy in the pit. (Homeboy, indeed!) Seriously, though, Tooth & Nail has made it its mission to spread the good word of positivity through music and, over the years, has expanded its empire by acquiring a series of subsidiary imprint labels.

For example, there's BEC Recordings, which hosts middle-of-the-road Christian-rock artists like **Hawk Nelson** and **Jeremy Camp**; Uprok Records, which specializes more in Christian hip-hop groups you probably haven't heard of unless you've attended the Holy Hip-Hop Night Camp in Clearwater, Florida; and Solid State Records, which has flourished in recent years thanks to the success of bands like **Demon Hunter**, **Norma Jean**, **Underoath**, and a bevy of other groups that perform wholesome metalcore, post-hardcore, and deathcore music. With Tooth & Nail constantly signing new bands (like crunk-rock Warped Tour vets **Family Force 5**) and pushing the envelope of what's considered "Christian music," the future is wide open for world domination. Hey, Newsboys, watch your backs.

DOS AND DON'TS OF CHRISTIAN ROCK

You just learned that Tooth & Nail Records is full of artists who study the Good Book—and I'm not talking about any ol' good book, like

---

* For the Fold's 2007 album *Secrets Keep You Sick*.

Everybody Hurts: An Essential Guide To Emo Culture. (Nod, nod, wink, wink.) But if I put a bunch of long-haired, heavily tattooed, burly metalcore dudes in a lineup, would you be able to tell which long-haired, heavily tattooed, burly metalcore dude was in a Christian band? If you're unsure, try considering the following dos and don'ts when figuring out if your fave band will be playing the Cornerstone Festival anytime soon.

DON'T USE THE LORD'S NAME IN VAIN

Our buddy J.C. doesn't like a potty mouth and most flag-waving Christian bands are more than happy to comply. That's why you'll be hard-pressed to find CDs with parental-advisory stickers or songs containing four-letter words, violent lyrical content, and references to naughty bits from bands in this God-respecting bunch. What you *will* find, however, is the unusually heated use of words like "shoot," "dang," and "crud," in addition to phrases like "heavens to Murgatroid" and "kiss my grits." Prepare accordingly.

DO SPEND SOME TIME IN PRAYER

Never underestimate the power of prayer, especially if you believe such acts of worship provide you with a direct line to the Man upstairs. Plus, unlike playing *Rock Band* or working out on a Nordic-Track machine, prayer can be done anywhere, anytime. For example, despite being on the road most of the year, band members from Underoath and Switchfoot can often be found partaking in prayer circles and Bible study when they're not performing. Now, if that doesn't deserve a gold star from God, I don't know what does.

DON'T HAVE SEX UNTIL YOU'RE MARRIED

Unlike some of our other commandments, this one is easier said than done—especially because so many band dudes (regardless of their religious affiliation) seem to only think with their pickle. Ah, the eternal struggle between secular and non-secular musicians. Take Pedro the Lion brain trust David Bazan. He's an admitted God-fearing Christian, yet he rebels against the Christian ideals of purity when he writes songs like "Second Best," which contains these lyrics: "The mattress creaks beneath / The symphony of misery and cum / Still we lie jerking back and forth / And blurring into one." Look, people, don't get me wrong: Sex is awesome, but when you're down with J.C., premarital sex isn't. Hey, if that's good enough for the Jonas Brothers, it's good enough for you.

DO SPREAD THE GOOD WORD

But try not to listen to that hunchback Pat Robertson who runs his mouth on *The 700 Club.* That guy's totally loco.

DON'T DRINK AND DO DRUGS

Watching addicts struggle with substance abuse might be captivating on shows like A&E's *Intervention*, but I'm pretty sure God isn't all that impressed by the crazy behavior of alcoholics and junkies, which is why so many Christian band members choose to keep it clean and go straight edge. Not only does the movement provide fodder for some killer Gorilla Biscuits–inspired tats, but its musicians never have to worry about getting themselves into a compromising position after hoovering up a shit-ton of blow during a poker game with Fat Mike. Speaking of, if you *do* happen to find yourself in a compromising position, say, after hoovering up a shit-ton of blow during a poker game with Fat Mike, it's best to admit your sins and repent. (*Cough*—Spencer Chamberlain from Underoath—*cough*.) After all, if there's one thing good Christians covet more than sobriety, it's the ability to forgive when someone effs up.

WHICH SEATTLE SCENESTER ARE YOU?

Luckily for the non-Jesus worshipping readership out there, Christian bands aren't the only groups that constitute the Seattle music scene. (Praise the Lord.) That said, let's take a look at the other types of scenesters you might encounter while picking up a halibut filet at Pike Place Market.

THE PREMATURELY BALDING HARD-CORE SCENESTER

Ah, male pattern baldness—what a bitch, especially for your typical hardcore/metalcore/screamo fan who wants nothing more than to headbang along to Botch with a full noggin of Crystal Gayle–esque flowing locks. Usually sporting a military jacket or Fred Perry zip-up, calf tattoos, and the occasional ill-fated fashion faux pas of white socks with black shoes, the Prematurely Balding Hardcore Scenester can often be found: (1) perusing the aisles at the Elliott Bay Book Company, anxiously trying to find a copy of *The Jungle* by Upton Sinclair; (2) waiting in line to see Flipper at the Fun House, despite complaining to the person in front of him that Krist Novoselic pales in comparison to previous bassist Bruno DeSmartass from punk band Bad Posture; or (3) shopping for a hat.

ON THEIR iPODS
Killswitch Engage
These Arms Are Snakes
Shadows Fall

SEATTLE, WASHINGTON

THE INTELLECTUAL INDIE SCENESTER

Though the group's moniker would suggest otherwise, there isn't an IQ prerequisite to qualify as an Intellectual Indie Scenester; instead, eligibility is based on whether or not Modest Mouse's *Lonesome Crowded West* appears in your iTunes playlist, how frequently you shop at Anthropologie, the number of David Foster Wallace tomes on your bookshelf, and whether you would find Ben Gibbard attractive if he didn't front Death Cab for Cutie. (For those Worishofer* sandal–wearing females, the answer, sadly, is yes.) You can often find members of this mock intelligentsia in the back of a Fleet Foxes gig regurgitating political views they heard on the latest episode of *The Colbert Report* or discussing Sam Rockwell's performance in the big-screen adaptation of Chuck Palahniuk's *Choke*.

ON THEIR iPODS
The Shins
The American Analog Set
Femmes de Paris, Vol. 1

---

* *n.* German brand of orthopedic sandals with a leather upper and cork sole. Often worn by nurses, Polish grandmothers, and Intellectual Indie Scenester girls in Belltown.

WISH YOU WERE HERE

THE GRUNGE HANGOVER SCENESTER

Much like Claymates and anyone related to Kim Kardashian, the Grunge Hangover Scenester is part of a sad, sad breed. When they're not mourning the death of flannel shirts, sock hats, and the Sub Pop Singles Club,* they're praying that all of these things will eventually make a comeback—and *soon*. Such scenesters barely listen to contemporary music created after 1996 (which is when Nirvana's posthumous *Live from the Muddy Banks of the Wishkah* was released), but make exception for anything involving grunge gods Dave Grohl or Chris Cornell. As far as I can tell, no matter how dated *Singles* gets or how many crappy albums the Vines release, there is no cure for the Grunge Hangover, which totally explains why Mudhoney still releases records.

ON THEIR iPODS
Soundgarden
The Melvins
Green River

_____

* In July 2008, Grunge Hangover Scenesters could at least cross one item off their wish list, because Sub Pop happily announced it would be reinstating its beloved Singles Club—at least for the twelve months that followed. For your sake, I hope you weren't too busy sewing together a new sock hat to subscribe.

SEATTLE, WASHINGTON

THE DENIM ROCK SCENESTER

Sorry, Jack White, but Detroit doesn't have the market cornered on garage rock and its disciples. In fact, thanks to Estrus Records, bands like the Makers, and a never-ending supply of dudes who want to look like a member of the Ramones (and/or *Rolling Stone*'s senior editor David Fricke), Seattle is comprised of a whole sect of Denim Rock Scenesters. You know the type: They're at least six-foot-five with a bowl cut hairdo and their uniform consists of a poor-man's tuxedo,* oversized sunglasses, black Converse high tops, and possibly clear glitter nail polish (depending on how much they're into T. Rex). There's a good chance they still live with their ex-girlfriend (because it's easier than mustering the energy to move out) and their idea of "interior decorating" is putting a drip candle in a Jack Daniel's bottle and turning on the black light. Caveat emptor: The Denim Rock Scenester is oftentimes charming, flirtatious, and affectionate, but you'll never know if it's because he likes your style or because he needs a new place to live.

ON THEIR iPODS
Murder City Devils
The Makers
Tight Bros from Way Back

---

* *n.* Outfit comprised of denim jacket and denim jeans. Often worn by Bon Jovi fans from New Jersey, fashionisto Carson Kressley from *Queer Eye for the Straight Guy*, and Denim Rock Scenesters who listen to *Little Steven's Underground Garage* on Sirius Satellite Radio.

<79>

THE GRUP SCENESTER

Named after an obscure *Star Trek* reference,* the word "grups" refers to the contraction of "grown-ups" and is mostly comprised of aging Gen Xers who are now in their mid- to late thirties and are dubiously staring down the rabbit hole of middle age. Faced with a slowing metabolism and an ever-expanding waistline, grups are more interested in leafing through the Room & Board catalog than trekking to Neumos to see Vampire Weekend. The name of the game is "nesting," and this scenester contingent is all about HGTV, trough sinks, and exposed brick walls. Often reminiscent of Jason Segel and Alyson Hannigan from *How I Met Your Mother*, grups couple up, and then the real fun begins, because it's only a matter of time before they spawn and are able to match the color of their BabyBjörn to the bisque leather interior of their Toyota Prius. *Finally.*

ON THEIR iPODS
The Postal Service
The Decemberists
Wilco

---

* In an episode entitled "Miri," from the first season of *Star Trek*, Captain Kirk & Co. visit a planet stricken by a deadly plague spread by grown-ups or "grups," as they're called. The only survivors are a group of children who have been left to live and govern themselves à la *Lord of the Flies*—minus the cannibalism and stuff.

HOW DO YOU KNOW WHEN YOU'VE GROWN GRUP?

Few music scenes seem to cater to the aging indie rocker better than Seattle. But how do you know when you've become, you know, one of them? It's pretty safe to say you've gone grup if . . .

. . . YOU SUBSCRIBE TO A NUMBER OF PERIODICALS DEDICATED TO EITHER THE ART OF MODERN ARCHITECTURE AND INTERIOR DESIGN OR RIDICULOUSLY ELABORATE DIY HOME IMPROVEMENT METHODS.

Are you a fan of stemless wine glasses? Have you signed up for pottery classes because you want to be the next Jonathan Adler? Do you feel like home décor can never be *too* modern? If so, then you probably take your design cues from cooler-than-cool mags like *Dwell*, *Juxtapoz*, and *i-D*. After all, for you're a grup, there's nothing more blissful on a Sunday afternoon than brewing a cup of loose-leaf tea, putting on a pair of James Perse lounge pants, and curling up on your Eames lounge chair (you know, the one you just purchased at Design Within Reach's floor sample sale) with the latest issue of *ReadyMade* magazine. Who knows when you'll need instruction on how to build your own butcher block, but if—or when—that day comes, you'll totally be prepared.

. . . WHEN EATING OUT WITH FRIENDS, YOU INSIST ON MEETING FOR TAPAS.*

Multicourse and à la carte meals are for plebeians with unsophisticated palates who have probably never even seen an episode of *Top Chef*. (Oh, the horror!) Thankfully, grups understand the smaller the plate, the better—especially when your dinner reservations fall somewhere between 9:00 and 11:00 p.m.

---

* *n.* Small-portioned, overpriced appetizers typically found in Spanish cuisine.

. . . THE LAST TIME YOU DID A STAGE DIVE WAS FOR THE LATEST CRATE & BARREL CATALOG.

Hell, if their silicone bakeware doesn't make you want to start a circle pit, I don't know what does.

. . . YOU GO GREEN.

It's not easy being green, but ever since you saw *An Inconvenient Truth* . . . Okay, scratch that . . . Ever since you *talked* to people who saw *An Inconvenient Truth*, you've been doing your part make your life more environmentally sound. You use reusable canvas bags when you go grocery shopping at Trader Joe's; you unplug your Bose Wave Music System when you're not using it; and you've even started taking public transportation to cut down on CO_2 emissions. Wait . . . *What?* Eff that. Grups don't take the bus. Have you ever been on the Metro, Al Gore? It smells like body odor and corned beef. Gag me with a spoon.

. . . YOU OWN A PARKA.

Yeah, I know it rains a ton in Seattle and everyone needs a hooded jacket[*] to help them brave the elements, but nothing screams "grup" like a quilted parka with a faux fur-lined hood. Preferred brands include the North Face, Mountain Hardwear, and Marmont—anything that would be worn by someone who has a carabiner key chain, shops at REI, and frequently takes kayaking trips to Ozette Lake. You should look like you just came back from surfing the tundra, even though you're not entirely sure where the tundra *is*.

MAPPING OUT SEATTLE

THE CHA CHA LOUNGE (1013 E PIKE ST., SEATTLE, WA 98122; HTTP://WWW.CHACHALOUNGE.COM)

Whether you've come to knock back one of their mind-bending margaritas or bask in the glory of purchasing a forty from the bar (yeah, you heard me right), the Cha Cha Lounge is one of Seattle's most beloved bars, especially for local musicians. In fact, many rockers—including members of Murder City Devils, the Melvins, and Modest Mouse—have manned the bar at one point or another.

CHOP SUEY (1325 E MADISON ST., SEATTLE, WA 98122; HTTP://WWW.CHOPSUEY.COM)

Originally known as a bar called the Breakroom, Chop Suey is quickly becoming one of Seattle's best places to see up-and-coming bands before they show up on *FNMTV* or something. The Asian-inspired décor is quirky and the lines to the bathroom are reasonable, but beware of the body heat—and odor—generated by a sold-out crowd in this small-capacity venue. I've got one word for you: heatstroke.

---

[*] True Seattle scenesters don't use umbrellas. Thems the rules. Apparently, it's better to be sopping wet than look like a poser. Talk about being too legit to quit.

EASY STREET RECORDS AND CAFÉ (4559 CALIFORNIA AVE. SW, SEATTLE, WA 98116; HTTP://EASYSTREETONLINE.COM)

If you're a member of the Experience Music Project and own at least one framed Charles Peterson photo, then there's a good chance you already frequent Easy Street Records on a regular basis. Lined with rows of CDs, tons of new and used vinyl, and lots of music memorabilia, Easy Street also has a stage that hosts intimate live sets by bands who happen to be passing through, like Sea Wolf, Kimya Dawson, and Pearl Jam (if you can believe it). Perhaps the best thing about this independent store is the fact that they offer a frequent buyer card that allows local audiophiles to get an eighteen-dollar credit after buying fifteen albums at any price.

Oh, and don't forget to stuff your face at the café downstairs. Not only will you get a kick out of items like the Horton Heat Hash and Culture Club Sandwich but you'll be licking your lips after inhaling these music-inspired dishes. In case you're looking for recommendations, I think the Soundgarden Burger can't be outshined. *Get it? Outshined?* It's a Soundgarden song, people. Work with me, here.

MIGHTY-O DONUTS (2110 N 55TH ST., SEATTLE, WA 98103; HTTP://WWW.MIGHTYO.COM)

Before settling into its current location, Mighty-O used to sell its delicious goods out of a mobile kitchen it would haul to flea markets and street fairs. Sure, doughnuts don't exactly qualify as a health food, but Mighty-O is all about sustainability and somehow manages to incorporate non-genetically modified, animal-free, organic, and vegan-friendly baking practices without sacrificing the deep-fried goodness of these lil' morsels. I recommend the Lemon Poppy and French Toast varieties.

THE REDWOOD (514 E HOWELL ST., SEATTLE, WA 98122)

Having only been open for a couple years, this Capitol Hill dive is slowly earning a solid rep amongst scenesters who are easily smitten by its rustic charm, signature bourbon sweet tea, and creamed-corn nuggets. The free peanuts are also a bonus, considering you can crack the shells and throw them on the floor without getting in trouble with the bar staff.

SHOWBOX MUSIC CLUB (1426 1ST AVE., SEATTLE, WA 98101; HTTP://WWW.SHOWBOXONLINE.COM)

How many clubs can brag that they played host to Al Jolson* *and* AFI? I'm betting not too many—except the Showbox, of course. Founded in 1939 as the Showbox Cabaret, the ballroom originally attracted the likes of those clamoring to hear legendary jazz musicians like Duke Ellington and Dizzy Gillespie. It would be another forty years, however, before the venue would emerge as the Pacific Northwest's center for new-wave activity thanks to booking local, national, and international bands like the Police, XTC, and the Jam. As new wave evolved into punk and alt-rock, the Showbox's event calendar quickly filled up with bills featuring the likes of Mudhoney, Pearl Jam, and the Screaming Trees. Then, when grunge took a backseat to indie bands at the turn of the century, the club kept on top of the scene by hosting then-unknown acts like Sleater-Kinney and Pretty Girls Make Graves.

Today, the venue has expanded its empire to Showbox at the Market, Showbox SoDo, and the Greenroom. With an upstairs bar and wide general admission set up, there isn't really a "bad seat" in the house. Plus, there's a photo booth to capture all sorts of regrettable pictures of yourself the next time Grand Archives plays here.

---

* Al Jolson was a Vaudeville performer who starred in the world's first talking picture in 1927, *The Jazz Singer*. He's considered by many music historians to be "the world's greatest entertainer" and perhaps the first-known rock star.

<85>

SONIC BOOM RECORDS (2209 NW MARKET ST., SEATTLE, WA 98107; HTTP://WWW.SONICBOOMRECORDS.COM)

With two locations (this one, in Capitol Hill, and another in Ballard), Sonic Boom has spent the past ten years as Seattle's most beloved neighborhood record store. Housing an extensive collection of vinyl, show posters, and gear, Sonic Boom took a slight hit in 2008 when they closed their Fremont location and a flood destroyed inventory in the store's vinyl annex, but that hasn't stopped the company from launching an impressive online store and booking performances by bands like Nada Surf and Earlimart at the two current locations.

Owned by Nabil Ayers (drummer for the Long Winters and founder of record label the Control Group) and Jason Hughes (former member of local bands Carmine and 6 Minute Mile), Sonic Boom is totally rooted in the local scene and has also played host to a number of quasi-famous employees, like Death Cab for Cutie bassist Nick Harmer. Oh, if you're at the Ballard store, also be sure to pop into the cuter-than-cute next-door boutique Velouria, which is owned by Hughes's better-half Tes de Luna.

STARBUCKS (1912 PIKE PL., SEATTLE, WA 98101; HTTP://WWW.STARBUCKS.COM)

Betcha didn't know that there are over fifteen thousand Starbucks stores in the world. . . . Or that Starbucks is partly named after Captain Ahab's first mate in *Moby Dick*. . . . Or even that the baristas have to complete a coffee master class before they can steam a single cup of milk. What did we do before the 'Bucks came into our lives? Let's not even think about it. Regardless of how many haters there are out there, I'm totally down to celebrate that the caffeine-fueled company got its start in Seattle. (Did you know *that*, Mr. Know-it-all?) Although the first Starbucks opened at 2000 Western Avenue in 1971, it moved five years later to the current Pike Place location, which is considered by the general coffee-drinking public to be the original locale of this mondo-chain.

THE FREMONT TROLL (N 36TH ST. AND AURORA AVE. N, SEATTLE, WA 98103)

Although the Fremont Troll isn't the most active Seattle resident (after all, he has been sitting on his tuckus for the past fifteen-plus years), he is one of the city's most beloved. Sculpted in 1991 by local artists, the Troll is nearly eighteen feet high and clutches a Volkswagen Beetle tightly in his left hand, which I can only imagine is a social commentary on consumerism, man vs. machine, or something equally esoteric. Over the years, the overgrown gnome has even inspired beers (Hale's Ales boasts a wicked Troll Porter), musicians (the Troll makes a guest appearance in Mudhoney's "Generation Spokesmodel" video), and filmmakers (although not credited on IMDB, the Troll has a cameo in *10 Things I Hate About You*). Damn, the Olsen twins must be pissed that their cousin is getting more work than they are.

A MOMENT OF SILENCE

THE CROCODILE CAFÉ (2201 3RD AVE. #803, SEATTLE, WA 98121)

When fans filled the Crocodile Café to catch sets from Dave Bazan and Fleet Foxes' Robin Pecknold and J. Tillman, they had no idea it would be the last time they would see a show at the beloved Belltown venue. In fact, nobody knew, but on the morning of December 16, 2007, owner Stephanie Dorgan left voice mails for her employees saying she wouldn't need them to show up for work anymore, locked

<87>

the doors to the venue, and closed up shop. In fact, up until spring 2008, you could still walk past the space, peer through the windows, and see the inside of the club exactly as it was left that last night in December. The Croc was officially a rock 'n' roll ghost town and not only were fans left without their favorite club, but they were also left without closure.

Dorgan originally opened the club in 1991 and it soon became a hotspot of grunge and alt-rock activity, attracting everyone from Pearl Jam to Cheap Trick to R.E.M. Dorgan even married R.E.M. guitarist Peter Buck in 1995 and the two of them ran the club together up until their divorce in 2006. However, in the years leading up to the couple's split, rumors of infighting and financial troubles seeped into the scene, and according to reports, Dorgan became more and more difficult to work with. Then, on December 4, 2007, an argument between Dorgan and talent booker Pete Greenberg—who had been at the club four years and was responsible for booking a new wave of local bands including the Cave Singers, Minus the Bear, and These Arms Are Snakes—resulted in his departure, which most cite as the beginning of the end. Luckily for Greenberg, his booking talents were quickly swallowed up by rival club Chop Suey, but the Croc never recovered—and neither has the Seattle music scene.

Spring 2000

After logging mucho miles with the Boca Raton punk band Vacant Andys and singing his heart out in Further Seems Forever, Pompano Beach's beloved Christian rockers, frontman Chris Carrabba breaks out on his own and plays his first solo show at Blue Note Records in Miami, Florida. Performing under the moniker Dashboard Confessional, Carrabba rips through a set of tear-jerking acoustic songs and inadvertently sparks a Swiss army romance with hardcore kids who had a soft spot for tender ballads about insomnia and split ends.

Suburban Florida

Littered with McMansions and a bunch of elderly people who shouldn't be allowed to have driver's licenses, the Florida suburbs were home to a scene that exploded during the late '90s, when local music came to prominence thanks to the success of a whole lot of soon-to-be pop-punk and post-hardcore legends who just so happened to have a soft-spot for melodramatic, acoustic ballads.

MUSIC PRIMER

There are some scenes that immediately strike a chord with thousands of disenfranchised teenagers. Then there are scenes like the one in suburban Florida, which, well, didn't exactly start off that way. Instead, it would take years for things to get rolling, because back in the mid-'80s, there really wasn't much to speak of when it came to the music scene in parts of Florida—unless you count a handful of hardcore bands like **Crucial Truth,**[*] which were gaining a smidgen of attention. Otherwise, Florida was better known for Latin-pop musicians like Gloria Estefan and Miami Sound Machine. (See, back before Ricky Martin shook his bonbon and Enrique Iglesias got his horrid mole removed, Gloria Estefan was as spicy as they came. She was like the J. Lo of her time—except she had actual musical talent. In fact, I wouldn't be surprised if your parents were listening to "Rhythm Is Gonna Get You" while you

_____
[*] Who, it bears mentioning, weren't getting all *that* much attention, but I digress.

were being conceived. If that thought alone is a little nauseating, hey, that's a pretty good indication of the effect her music could have on most people.)

Anyway, things finally began to improve some ten years later, when an honest-to-goodness punk scene began developing in Gainesville, a small college town about an hour outside of Jacksonville. Arguably, the first band to gain notoriety from the area was **Less Than Jake**, a jokey band of merry punkers who thought everything sounded better with horns, which eventually led to the band's signature ska-punk style. Never one to take themselves too seriously, LTJ's first album, 1995's *Pezcore*, was inspired by a mutual love of Pez shared between bassist Roger Manganelli and drummer Vinnie Fiorello, and included fan favorites like "Liquor Store" and "Johnny Quest Thinks We're Sellouts"; the band then followed up that masterpiece with a bevy of beloved 7-inches (like *All My Best Friends Are Metalheads* and *Crash Course in Being an Asshole*), plus an EP of *Grease* covers. I wish I were kidding.

While Fiorello and his bandmates were singing "Summer Nights" at VFW halls up and down the coast, a much more influential group was beginning to take shape back in Gainesville. Named after a Charles Bukowski novel, **Hot Water Music** almost instantly started to define the scene with its unique approach to post-hardcore, which happened to be influenced by the band's impressive ability to grow facial hair and drink whiskey at two in the afternoon, in addition to vocalist Chuck Ragan's sandpaper singing style, which sounded like he had just finished gargling with a bunch of marbles. Florida had never seen—or heard—anything like them before. But after HWM, everyone in the Gainesville scene looked that way, including the male members of **Discount**, a local pop-punk group that also loved drinking but, quite clearly, didn't have the same passion for things like beards. The one thing that really set Discount apart, though, was Alison Mosshart, quite possibly the only female musician in the Gainesville scene at that point. Understandably, spending a considerable amount of time around burly, drunk dudes can have some adverse affects on a girl, which may explain why Mosshart eventually left Florida for London, where she changed her name to "VV," started a new band named **the Kills**, and began appearing in hipster fashion magazines alongside Terry Richardson.*

Before Mosshart skipped town, though, Discount began playing out in the suburbs with bands like **Shai Hulud**, a metal-leaning hardcore act that loved ridiculously dramatic song titles. Shai Hulud also apparently loved scouting middle schools for new band members, seeing that its first singer, Chad Gilbert, was all of fourteen by the time he joined the band and, no joke, had to make the band's roadie his legal guardian in order to go out on tour. A few years later, Gilbert split from Shai Hulud and began playing with another local band, **New Found**

---

* Born 1965. Richardson is hailed by the fashion elite as an über-talented photographer known for developing a style in which every photo he takes looks like it was shot on the set of a '70s porno with a disposable camera. To illustrate his humility, Richardson is often know to place himself alongside his subject in any campaign he shoots. What a guy.

Glory. In the same way Hot Water Music best represented the scene in Gainesville, New Found Glory was the one group that completely summed up what it was like in the 'burbs. Most of their songs were about teenage angst and girls and . . . well, that's it.

Then again, for New Found Glory and many of its musical peers in Florida, that was the point. After years of everyone taking their "art" so seriously in punk and hardcore bands, there were many groups in the area that were now prepared to make complete asses out of themselves. In turn, it became fairly common to see New Found Glory's 700-pound bassist perform shirtless at shows, or catch **the Vacant Andys**, an admittedly goofy group that included future **Further Seems Forever** and **Dashboard Confessional** frontman Chris Carrabba, putting on a sloppy set at various coffeehouses around Boca Raton. Yet another member of this fun loving new wave of bands was Jacksonville's **Yellowcard**, which, for the first three years of its career seemed like one continuous joke. Granted, some people might argue that its entire career has been one continuous joke, but back then, that was the idea. This was a band, after all, that released an album called *Midget Tossing* and asked an orchestra nerd they knew from high school to join as their violinist. They had to be kidding, right?

Actually, they weren't, and over the next few years, the Florida music scene changed significantly. Eventually, Yellowcard moved to Los Angeles and wrote a half-assed concept record about Hollywood, while New Found Glory and Dashboard Confessional churned out the kind of records that were targeted at soccer moms who drove Honda Odysseys and

TiVoed *The Amazing Race*. In the meantime, new bands like **Anberlin** and **Underoath** started to reclaim the suburban scene and serve up rock and screamo with a heavy helping of spirituality. In fact, the only thing the members of those groups loved more than flat-irons and complicated G-Star jackets, was the Man Upstairs. Thus, they routinely made a point of telling people this at their live shows. As this was happening, the scene back in Gainesville also started to shift with the rising popularity of folk-punk acts like **Army of Ponch** and, more important, **Against Me!**, a band so unbelievably stern that it actually inspired former fans to picket outside of its shows when it signed to a major label in 2006.

So, what's the scene like today? Well, even if you're a non-Christian and would rather get a pedicure than participate in a protest, Florida bands have got you covered. First, there are the good ol' boy rockers in **the Red Jumpsuit Apparatus**. Sure, lead singer Ronnie Winters might have prettier hair than your girlfriend, but the dude can belt it out like a bat out of hell. (Watch out, Meatloaf.) Relative newcomers like **We the Kings** and **Mayday Parade** are earning cred with the Warped Tour crowd, thanks to dreamy-looking band members, catchy melodies, and really obnoxious T-shirt designs. Finally, critical darlings like **Iron and Wine** and **Black Kids** are hypnotizing the indie masses, while **Evergreen Terrace** and **Casey Jones** are keeping it real by carrying on Florida's long-standing hardcore punk tradition. Florida might be a state full of old people, but the suburban music scene has never been younger and fresher.

LABEL CONSCIOUS

When it comes to the scene in suburban Florida, two record labels have helped shape the musical landscape into what it is today—**No Idea** and **Fueled by Ramen**. Like many other independent record labels that came before it, No Idea started out in 1985 as a fanzine put together by high school friends Var Thelin and Ken Coffelt. By 1989, with six issues under their belts, Thelin & Co. came up with the brilliant idea to include a 7-inch with each magazine and ended up putting out music by bands like **the Doldrums** and **Crimpshrine**. However, it wasn't until 1996 that No Idea started exclusively releasing records and built an impressive roster of bands that included **Dillinger Four**, **Hot Water Music**, and **Small Brown Bike**.

Today, the label is best known for being the launching pad for Anarchist rockers **Against Me!** and a bunch of other beard-punk bands like **Army of Ponch**, **Bomb the Music Industry!**, and **the Gaslight Anthem**. Fans of these bands are pretty easy to spot because they're usually sporting some kind of facial hair (regardless of gender), have a tendency to burst into drunken sing-alongs (regardless of whether they're drunk), and rock an eye patch with a tendency to exclaim "Arrr, matey" (regardless of pirate decent) whenever they get together in groups larger than three.

In contrast, while fans of **Planes Mistaken for Stars** were clamoring for No Idea test pressings in the late '90s, another independent label was starting to bubble below the surface in Tampa. Started by **Less Than Jake** drummer Vinnie Fiorello and friend John Janick in 1996, Fueled by Ramen was a small pop-punk label known for releases from then-underground bands like **Discount**, **Jimmy Eat World**, and **Recover**. However, it would be another seven years before FBR would release the album responsible for changing the direction of the label—and the scene in general: **Fall Out Boy**'s *Take This to Your Grave*.

From that point on, Fueled by Ramen became more than just your everyday indie record label; it became a brand name that would soon be marketed to the masses, thanks to the success of bands like **the Academy Is . . .**, **Gym Class Heroes**, and **Panic at the Disco**. Suddenly, the underdogs were becoming heroes of the scene and selling millions of albums along the way. Always evolving, FBR gave Fall Out Boy's Pete Wentz his own imprint, Decaydance, and major label Atlantic Records bought a stake in FBR, as well. Unfortunately, not happy with the direction the label was taking, Fiorello stepped down in 2006 and left Janick to run the show with newcomers like **Cute Is What We Aim For**, **the Cab**, **Cobra Starship**, and a bunch of other bands starting with the letter "C." Time will tell if Fueled by Ramen and its roster will survive the scene's next wave of bands—or be on that wave's crest.

ESSENTIAL SUBURBAN FLORIDA ALBUM GUIDE

If your music collection is already filled with albums from the above bands, congrats! You're ahead of the game. If you're hanging your head in shame because none of the above bands are in your collection, all is not lost. Amazon.com exists for a reason. Before you beat yourself up too much, put the following essential albums in your cart and I guarantee your mood will improve immediately!

HOT WATER MUSIC: *FUEL FOR THE HATE GAME*
(NO IDEA, 1997)

WHAT YOU NEED TO KNOW: After Hot Water Music released its debut back in 1996, the band actually broke up briefly. Thankfully, the hiatus didn't stick, and it wasn't long until it recorded this landmark album and began churning out sweat-soaked live sets at just about every vegan potluck and punk-rock fest in the country. By doing so, the band became even more popular than it ever imagined and managed to wait another ten years before calling it quits for good.

WHAT MAKES IT ESSENTIAL: During its career, the band recorded a handful of albums for various different record labels, but *Fuel for the Hate Game* remains its most essential record, at least among its diehard fans. In fact, in the winter of 2008, when the band decided to play its final shows together, it wasn't uncommon to see a whole lot of chubby dudes in their thirties not only hugging, but crying, whenever the group launched into "Freightliner."

SHAI HULUD: *HEARTS ONCE NOURISHED WITH HOPE AND COMPASSION* (REVELATION, 1997)

WHAT YOU NEED TO KNOW: This was the only record that this highly combustible band made with its original lineup, which featured fourteen-year-old Chad Gilbert on vocals. Despite the fact that Gilbert was still too young to shave, he somehow managed to sound like a middle-aged serial killer while screaming over soon-to-be hardcore classics like "A Profound Hatred of Man."

WHAT MAKES IT ESSENTIAL: One reason this album remains so important is that some of the underground's most popular metal bands—like As I Lay Dying and Unearth—still cite it as an influence. Another reason it's so essential, is because it's the only album Shai Hulud made before it found itself on the verge of breaking up which, some seventy-two different lineups later, is where it *still* finds itself today.

DISCOUNT: *CRASH DIAGNOSTIC* (NEW AMERICAN DREAM, 2000)

WHAT YOU NEED TO KNOW: Produced by former Jawbox vocalist/guitarist J. Robbins, *Crash Diagnostic* is the swan song for a band that imploded before reaching its full potential. Discount formed back in 1995, when its members were still in junior high, and over the next five years, it would unknowingly establish itself as one of the most influential post-punk bands out there, thanks to perfectly crafted songs like "Broken to Blue" and "Age of Spitting."

WHAT MAKES IT ESSENTIAL: Discount disbanded in 2000, soon after releasing *Crash Diagnostic*, and elusive singer Alison Mosshart moved to England to start the Kills with Jamie Hince, a rail-thin anarcho-punk and Kate Moss boy toy. As for the four other members of Discount. . . . Well, they went back to their jobs shipping boxes at a local warehouse. Sorry, but these aren't all Cinderella stories people.

DASHBOARD CONFESSIONAL: *THE PLACES YOU HAVE COME TO FEAR THE MOST* (VAGRANT, 2001)

WHAT YOU NEED TO KNOW: With the release of *The Places You Have Come to Fear the Most*, Dashboard Confessional confirmed that

quiet was the new loud when it came to hardcore music. Reminiscent of Elliott Smith on Redbull, DC brain trust Chris Carrabba bared his lovelorn soul in songs like "Screaming Infidelities" and "The Best Deceptions," often causing audiences to sing louder than the former Further Seems Forever frontman at live shows. **WHAT MAKES IT ESSENTIAL:** Sporting a swoon-worthy baby pomp and more tattoos than an episode of *L.A. Ink,* Carrabba immediately became a shaman for all broken-hearted youths with asymmetrical haircuts who never thought they had a voice—or just never decided to use it for singing *"her hair is everywhere"* at the top of their lungs.

NEW FOUND GLORY: *STICKS AND STONES* (DRIVE-THRU, 2002)

WHAT YOU NEED TO KNOW: Known up until this release as one of pop-punk's best-kept secrets, New Found Glory exploded into the mainstream after fellow Warped Tour alumnus Good Charlotte made it safe for tattoos and Liberty spikes to appear on MTV. Sure, Jordan Pundik's signature nasal and high-pitched vocals are an acquired taste, but they make songs like "My Friends over You" and "Head on Collision" instant stage-diving classics.

WHAT MAKES IT ESSENTIAL: Besides the fact that the members of NFG have more hardcore cred than the average record store clerk at Wayward Council, *Sticks and Stones* reminds me of a time when pop-punk was the perfect musical expression of teen angst—mostly because it was actually written by a bunch of teenagers.

POISON THE WELL: *YOU COME BEFORE YOU* (ATLANTIC, 2003)

WHAT YOU NEED TO KNOW: Back in the early 2000s, all it took was a pair of Diesel jeans and a really annoying dude screaming in the background of your songs to score a record deal. In turn, all sorts of music industry insiders thought this Miami-based screamo band was going to be the next big thing—and that, furthermore, *this* was the album that was going to break it into the mainstream. Guess what? They were wrong.

WHAT MAKES IT ESSENTIAL: In the end, "screamo" basically became this decade's answer to electronica (Remember when the Sneaker Pimps were gonna be huge, too?) and Poison the Well was eventually dropped by its label. In Florida, however, it remains the heavy-leaning band to namedrop, especially if you are in an up-and-coming hardcore band and are being interviewed by a webzine.

LESS THAN JAKE: *ANTHEM* (SIRE, 2003)

WHAT YOU NEED TO KNOW: Less Than Jake first made a name for themselves—both in Gainesville and around the country—when bands like Skankin' Pickle were all the rage.* Shortly thereafter, though, many new-school, ska-punk fans realized that wearing checkered suspenders and creepers made them look like really tall idiots; thus, many of the genre's more popular bands called it a day. Thankfully, the Jake soldiered on with the sound of *Anthem*.

WHAT MAKES IT ESSENTIAL: What makes it essential? Can you name one other band from the mid-'90s ska boom that made its best album ten years later? I didn't think so. Laugh at their goofy stage antics and immature lyrics all you want, but you can't help but admire their tenacity and dedication.

YELLOWCARD: *OCEAN AVENUE* (CAPITOL, 2003)

WHAT YOU NEED TO KNOW: Up until the early 2000s, Jacksonville's biggest musical export was Limp Bizkit. *Great*. However, while

* No, seriously. There was a time when Skankin' Pickle was all the rage. Stop laughing.

Fred Durst was busy updating his inane Xanga blog, the members of Yellowcard were crafting a perfect pop-punk postcard of life in the Florida 'burbs. The result is 2003's *Ocean Avenue*, which not only launched frontman Ryan Key as an unexpected emo sex symbol but proved that violins are actually more punk rock than you think.

WHAT MAKES IT ESSENTIAL: Built on the success of singles like "Ocean Avenue" and "Only One," Yellowcard ended up walking away with the MTV2 Award at the 2004 MTV Music Video Awards, which is memorable for two reasons: (1) The 'Card beat out cooler bands like Franz Ferdinand, Modest Mouse, and the Yeah Yeah Yeahs, and (2) when accepting said reward, Key broke down like a little girl, thus enforcing the stereotype that emo types are a bunch of crybabies.

UNDEROATH: *THEY'RE ONLY CHASING SAFETY* (SOLID STATE, 2004)

WHAT YOU NEED TO KNOW: Before releasing this album, Underoath was a bunch of schlubby Christian hardcore kids whom barely anyone outside of their hometown of Tampa had ever heard of. But after *Safety* came out, they suddenly morphed into a real-deal rock band, complete with flat-ironed hair and, in the case of drummer Aaron Gillespie, the kind of dramatic weight loss that made you wonder if the dude was living solely off of Tic Tacs.

WHAT MAKES IT ESSENTIAL: By getting a crapload of airplay for the video for "It's Dangerous Business Walking out Your Front Door" on MTV2 and Fuse, Underoath was soon put in a position to play in front of bigger and bigger crowds. Oftentimes during these performances, Underoath would give shout-outs to its main man, J.C., without whom they would be nothing but a bunch of geeky Guitar Center salespeople with adult braces. Their collective love of God, however, isn't what makes this album essential; instead, it's that they somehow managed to convert crowds at rowdy punk-rock festivals like the Warped Tour and no one in the audience threw their shoes at them.

SUBURBAN FLORIDA

<102>

AGAINST ME! *SEARCHING FOR A FORMER CLARITY* (FAT WRECK CHORDS, 2005)

WHAT YOU NEED TO KNOW: After nearly ten years as a band, Against Me! had played countless squats and logged thousands of miles in a smelly tour van, only to watch the majority of its friends abandon the punk scene for life on a major label. As a result, the four of them decided to write this quasi-concept album, which was more or less about how they would never, under any circumstance, sell out to the Man. Ummm, about that last part . . .

WHAT MAKES IT ESSENTIAL: As it turned out, Against Me! ended up signing on the dotted line no less than a year after this album was released. As a result, practically everyone in Gainesville began to lose their shit, resulting in a whole lot of online trash-talking and even one dude getting punched in the face. (See "Mapping Out Suburban Florida" section for more details.)

WHICH SUBURBAN FLORIDA SCENESTER ARE YOU?

After perusing the eloquently worded essential album guide detailed above, it's easy to see that the musical community in Florida is incredibly eclectic. After all, this is the same scene that can take credit for inspiring punk troubadours, underage hardcore kids, and goofy ska fans alike. So where exactly do you fit in? That's a good question, but not one that can be properly answered until you examine the five major scenesters that currently exist in Florida's musical landscape.

THE HEARTFELT ACOUSTIC SCENESTER

If you find yourself consistently pushing your MySpace URL on people at parties or saying things like, "Dude, you've *got* to listen to this new demo I posted called 'The Wicked Tyranny of Young Hearts'; it's awesome," then this is probably the category that suits you best. Mostly male and underfed, your average Heartfelt Acoustic Scenester is constantly waging a war against detractors who mock his sensitivity. So what if he watches *Dr. Phil* and subscribes to *Cosmo*? It's only to better acquaint himself with the fabulous females in his life. (They're often misunderstood, you know.) Why should it matter that he has a man-crush on Ryan Reynolds or that he carries around a small notepad in his back jean pocket so he can write down his feelings at a moment's notice? Don't mistake his tenderness and gentility for frailty and weakness. The Heartfelt Acoustic Scenester is all man—at least that's what he keeps telling himself when the cashier at Publix says, "Would you like the receipt in the bag, miss?"

ON THEIR iPODS
Dashboard Confessional
Iron and Wine
Secondhand Serenade

THE FRAT PUNK SCENESTER

Have you ever tailgated in the Dolphin Stadium parking lot while blasting the first New Found Glory record? Do you buy most of your wardrobe from stores like Abercrombie & Fitch, Hollister, and American Eagle? Are you still trying to translate the Chinese letters you got tattooed on your chest during spring break last year (though you've got it narrowed down to "Free as a Bird" or "Watch Out, Bird Poop")? If you answered "yes" to any—or all—of the above, allow me to induct you into the Frat Punk Scenester brotherhood. As opposed to other fraternities, though, no one is going to test your loyalty by forcing you to participate in the elephant walk.* There's no hazing necessary to become a Frat Punk Scenester. Possessing a hideous wardrobe and obnoxious personality is punishment enough.

ON THEIR iPODS
Yellowcard
New Found Glory
O.A.R.

---

* If you don't already know what this is, then let's keep it that way. Trust me. You're better off.

THE SKA PUNK SCENESTER

Are you in your mid-thirties, still sporting second-hand thrift-store suits, and driving the kind of run-down vintage car that hasn't passed an E-Check in fifteen years? When you go to a local show, do you oftentimes find yourself standing in the back, complaining about how "all these pussy emo bands" are "ruining the scene"? If so, then you are probably a Ska Punk Scenester, and let's face it, you are part of a dying breed. Take pride in that fact. But you know, maybe not *too* much pride. After all, you still have to go home at night and listen to ska records, which isn't something I'd wish on my worst enemy.

ON THEIR iPODS
Less Than Jake
Madness
The Mighty Mighty Bosstones

THE MALL PUNK SCENESTER

In order to properly diagnose you, I'd appreciate it if you could answer a three-part quiz:

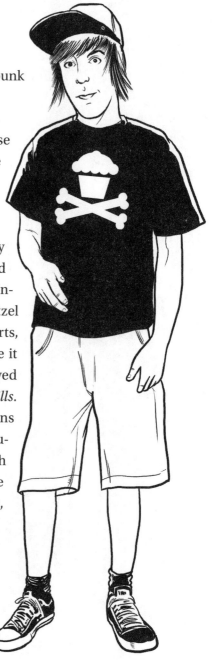

1. Do you like pop-punk?
2. Do you like the mall?
3. Do you like talking about pop-punk *at* the mall?

If you answered yes to any of these questions, then you are a bonafide Mall Punk Scenester and, hands down, you are one of the most ubiquitous scenesters I'll be outlining in the section. Take a stroll through any local shopping center in Florida and you're bound to see a handful of kindred spirits loitering in front of Pretzel Time, wearing baggy Dickies shorts, and loudly discussing how awesome it was to hear We the Kings being played during last night's episode of *The Hills*. For better or worse, these are the fans who helped introduce the Florida music scene to the mainstream, which was not exactly embraced by the next group I'll be discussing here, which is . . .

ON THEIR iPOD
All Time Low
Boys Like Girls
Mayday Parade

THE BEARD PUNK SCENESTER

. . . ah, yes, the Beard Punk Scenesters. These often-hairy scene luminaries couldn't be more different from the group described above. For one, they wouldn't be caught dead at the mall. No, they'd rather spend their time hanging at dingy squats in Gainesville, even though their parents live in the affluent Haile Plantation section of the city. Recreational activities aside, there's another way to properly identify if you are, in fact, a Beard Punk Scenester. Three words: You smell bad. *Really* bad. You see, despite the fact that most Beard Punk Scensters work at their local co-op (where, last time I checked, they carry things like "shampoo" and "soap"), the majority of them choose to smell like wet garbage covered in baby spit-up that's spent the past week marinating in the hot sun. Dude, even the description makes me wanna dry heave. So, if your odor is so nasty that it offends the nasal passages of homeless people, then there's a pretty good chance that you're a Beard Punk Scenester.

ON THEIR iPODS
The Draft
Defiance, Ohio
Against Me!

SUBURBAN FLORIDA

ALL FEST UP

Burly Beard Punk Scenesters—and their designated drivers—who complain that the scene in suburban Florida is dwindling should look no further than the annual Fest, which is held in Gainesville each year and features over 180 punk, hardcore, and emo bands. Even if you have no idea what bands are on No Idea Records, you have to mark this on your calendar, like, *now* if you want to fit in with the Florida scene. With the limitless flow of alcohol and wet T-shirts, it's just like spring break in Daytona Beach, except it's in Gainesville. . . . And it's in the fall. . . . And the wet T-shirts are on a bunch of overweight dudes who can't keep their Pabst tallboys in the can while fist-pumping to the Riverboat Gamblers.

<109>

So maybe the spring break analogy was a stretch, but the Fest draws fans from all over the country (and possibly the world) to watch the bands, eat endless amounts of barbecue, and compete for the title of Dude Who Owns Most Extensive Hot Water Music Vinyl Collection (but Still Lives Above His Parents' Garage). Shows at the Fest take place at a bunch of proper venues including 1982, the Venue, the Atlantic, Market Street Pub, the Side Bar, Common Grounds, the Pontiac, and Second Street Bakery, in addition to various unsanctioned houses, apartments, basements, parking lots, and abandoned cardboard refrigerator boxes.

Although the Fest might not boast the big headliners of traveling festivals like the Vans Warped Tour or Projekt Revolution, fans attending the annual Gainesville getaway will inevitably go batshit-crazy for the chance to see bands like Against All Authority and Small Brown Bike rip it up. We know. "Again All *Who*? Small Brown *What*?" Okay, so I'm not exactly talking about household names, but there's obviously a huge audience for this stuff or else the Fest wouldn't be getting bigger every year. So pass the Blatz and shut your piehole. Dude, Paint It Black is about to play!

MAPPING OUT SUBURBAN FLORIDA

ALL SAINTS CAFÉ (903 RAILROAD AVE., TALLAHASSEE, FL 32310; HTTP://WWW .MYSPACE.COM/ALLSAINTSCAFE)

Grab your cameras, Against Me! enthusiasts, because you'll want to document every nook and espresso cranny of All Saints Café. Why? Well, this coffeehouse is only *the* place where Tom Gabel allegedly slammed some dude's neck down on a counter after said dude hassled the frontman for ripping down a defaced

Against Me! flyer from the wall. Then, while you and your friends re-enact the scene—complete with a perfectly choreographed headlock and head-butt routine—try the java here. I hear it's delish.

BACKBONE MUSIC (61 SE 4TH AVE., DELRAY BEACH, FL 33483; HTTP://WWW.MYSPACE.COM/BACKBONEMUSIC)

Voted "Best Record/CD Store 2007" by the local *New Times*, Back-bone Music features an extensive CD and vinyl collection—at least by Florida standards. In addition to in-store performances, it's also nice to know that since Backbone opened in 2005, none of its stock has been sitting on the shelf for decades, like at other record stores. Face it, there's nothing worse than *finally* finding that *Zaireeka* box set by the Flaming Lips and having it covered with an inch-think film of dirt, dust, and dead bugs from having sat untouched since its release in 1997.

CHURCHILL'S PUB (5501 NE 2ND AVE., MIAMI, FL 33127; HTTP://WWW.CHURCHILLSPUB.COM)

Churchill's Pub brings a little bit of jolly ol' England to Southern Florida—especially when the club hosts bands like Boy Prostitute and Johnny Sex Fuck, which I hear are *huge* in Europe. Joking aside, Churchill's is considered Florida's version of CBGB, though somehow I doubt the late Hilly Kristal would've ever hosted sticky stuff women's wrestling at the NYC punk haven.

COMMON GROUNDS (210 SW 2ND AVE., GAINESVILLE, FL 32601; HTTP://WWW.COMMONGROUNDSLIVE.COM)

If you're looking for a simple cup of Joe, try Starbucks. Ignore the misleading moniker because Common Grounds is anything but a coffeehouse. Instead, it's a bichin' music venue where you can catch hometown heroes like Army of Ponch, the Draft, and Jabberwocky share the stage with other national punk, hardcore, and indie acts. Open seven days a week, the club is eighteen and over unless accom-panied by a parent. (Kind of a bummer, I know, but not if your pops is willing to sit through a set from Look Mexico.) A word to the wise: Beware that you're entering Tom Gabel country here so make sure you don't hold your next anti–Against Me! protest out front or you're in for an ass-whooping. Don't say I didn't warn you.

DOCKSIDE BOARDWALK (1100 6TH AVENUE S, NAPLES, FL 34102)

Every Fourth of July, this is the spot in Northern Florida where you are likely to find a collection of teenage punks and sixtysomething grandpas watching the fireworks go off. Now, while patriotism is nice and all, that's not the only reason the Boardwalk has become a Florida landmark. No, as it turns out, this is also where Against Me!'s Tom Gabel was cuffed, for the first time, at the age of fourteen, and where, after resisting arrest, he had to be hog-tied by the cops. What? Did they call him a "sell out" or something?

F.I.A. CLOTHING (815 W UNIVERSITY AVE., GAINESVILLE, FL 32601)

Sorry, dudes, but this boutique is strictly for those with XX chromosomes—unless you're, like, a cross-dresser or something. To that I say, hells yeah, sister mister! F.I.A. (which stands for "Future Iconoclasts of America") opened in 2005 and has been stocking the cutest of the cute in new and vintage apparel and accessories ever since.

INERTIA RECORDS AND BOOKS (820 LOMAX ST., JACKSONVILLE, FL 32204; HTTP://DEADTANK.WORDPRESS.COM)

Over the past couple years, Jacksonville has become a breeding ground for some of the scene's most buzz-worthy bands, like Yellowcard and the Red Jumpsuit Apparatus. Inertia Records and Books might stock albums by these bands (and more!), but I'm betting you won't find any Ryan Key or Ronnie Winters superfans working behind the counter. If you want to see something really special, ask for a copy of Brazilian hardcore band Discarga's *Que Venha Abaixo* 7-inch EP and watch your indie cred soar.

SUBURBAN FLORIDA

JACK RABBITS (1528 HENDRICKS AVE., JACKSONVILLE, FL 32207; HTTP://WWW.JACKRABBITSONLINE.COM)

Located across the street from the San Marco Library in Jacksonville, Jack Rabbits is hardly your destination for peace and quiet while you complete your problem sets for calculus. Instead, it's *the* premiere venue for Northeast Florida and features live music nearly every day of the week. Though the joint primarily caters to those chomping at the bit for emo and hardcore, if you're lucky, you might be able to catch something a little more, uh, unique—like Man-Sized Rat, a local metal band that does the occasional Prince cover. You can't get more unique than that, right?

RAG JUNKIE (931 N MONROE ST., TALLAHASSEE, FL 32303; HTTP://WWW.RAG-JUNKIE.COM)

Just because you're going to a house show at the Good Idea House with 150 of your closest—and sweatiest—friends, doesn't mean that you have to look like a hobo. Instead, stop by and pick up a killer baby-doll dress and a pair of Oh Deer heels. Besides looking fierce, you won't end up breaking the bank, because nothing in the store is over a hundred dollars!

THE REVOLUTION (200 W BROWARD BLVD., FORT LAUDERDALE, FL 33312; HTTP://WWW.JOINTHEREVOLUTION.NET)

Located in downtown Fort Lauderdale, the Revolution features a two-thousand-person capacity outdoor stage where bands like Fall Out Boy, Angels and Airwaves, and Silverstein have ripped it up over the years. On nights when the venue isn't hosting shows, the indoor club boasts two bars, a VIP section, and room for more than a thousand of your closest friends to bump and grind to your favorite Fergie remix.

WAYWARD COUNCIL (807 W UNIVERSITY AVE., GAINESVILLE, FL 32601; HTTP://MEMBERS.TRIPOD.COM/WAYWARD_COUNCIL)

Gainesville's Wayward Council is the epitome of punk's DIY philosophy. Sure, it seems like locals are constantly holding benefit shows in order to help the store make rent, but that's because this creative co-op is run 100 percent by volunteers and boasts a not-for-profit mission statement, which results in no boss, no wages, and, well, sometimes no money for rent. Beware, tourists: Anything goes at Wayward Council, so before you walk inside to buy a piece of feminist prose or something, prepare yourself, because you might see someone doing a keg-stand by the front counter or a couple copulating in the back corner. Let's just say that both have been known to happen.

A MOMENT OF SILENCE

CHEERS (2490 SW 17TH AVE., MIAMI, FL 33145)

Cheers may've only been around for a couple years (1995–1997, roughly), but the venue made a lasting impression on anyone who ever caught a show there, got in a brawl at the gas station across the street, or snagged a slice of pizza from Casola's in between sets. Owned and operated by a middle-aged woman named Gay, who just happened to be, well, *gay*, Cheers was just a quick drive down 95 South from neighboring cities like Fort Lauderdale (a mere thirty minutes, depending on traffic) and hosted the best hardcore bills in the area.

Back in the day, it wouldn't be out of the ordinary to see a baby-faced Chad Gilbert playing bass in Tension one night and rocking out the next in a fledgling pop-punk band called Last Minute (which included members Ryan Primack and Chris Hornbrook, who would go on to form Poison the Well). All shows were all-ages, and after earning a solid rep in the scene, it wasn't long before the dingy club became a destination for then up-and-coming bands like Blink-182, AFI, and the Promise Ring. New Found Glory even played its first show there on June 11, 1997, to a crowd of fewer than fifty people; unfortunately, it wasn't but a short time later that Cheers ended up closing its doors for good.

Today, a Quiznos Sub Shop stands where Cheers used to be. Sure, you might not be able to catch Anal Cunt playing there, but if you go across the street to the Exxon station, there's still a good chance that some thug could smash you over the head with the Club. Ah, memories.

August 8, 2000

Taking Back Sunday plays Garden City Bowl with Thisyearsmodel, Now She's Gone, Error Type 11, and At the Drive-In. Its set takes place on the carpeted walkway behind the lanes and nearly 250 people cram into the space to catch a glimpse of the band's singer Antonio Longo. There are so many kids clamoring to catch a peak that some brave souls even scale the bowling lockers when there isn't any more standing room. Although the band has no label, no album, and nearly no reputation outside of Long Island, the at-capacity crowd sings along with Longo's every word.

Long Island

If there is one thing that this ultra-suburban area has contributed to the shape of underground rock, it's young male angst. From the tough-guy hardcore bands that came up in the late '90s to the more sensitive locals who helped bring emo to the mainstream in the early 2000s, let's examine this New York 'burb's lasting influence on the surrounding music scene.

MUSIC PRIMER

Long Island—pronounced "Lawn Guyland" by anyone with a native tongue—has long been a hotbed of musical activity, boasting such high-profile natives as Twisted Sister's Dee Snider and AM-rocker Eddie Money, who have both sold millions of records and, oddly enough, spawned offspring cast in the first season of MTV's *Rock the Cradle.** (Coincidence? I think not.) However, it wasn't until the late '90s that this affluent area's underground rock scene attracted the kind of attention last garnered by the Pacific Northwest around the time flannel—and Nirvana—exploded.

The modern-day incarnation of the Long Island music scene truly begins with **Glassjaw**, an experimental post-hardcore band

---

* Rumor has it that the original name of this show was *I Have a Famous Last Name*, but producers worried that it would be confused with another MTV series, called *I Want a Famous Face*, which also feature anonymous wannabes besmirching the natural talent of legitimate celebrities.

led by a pint-sized vocal powerhouse named Daryl Palumbo, a Catholic straight-edge kid from Bellmore who suffered from a gnarly digestive disease and supposedly hated girls, both of which inspired songs on the band's Roadrunner Records debut, *Everything You Ever Wanted to Know About Silence*. Despite more than a dozen members revolving in and out of the lineup over the next ten years, the band managed to release one more album (2002's *Worship and Tribute*) before going on hiatus (more about that later). It was during this time off from the band that Palumbo listened to a ton of Squeeze records, hooked up with producer Dan the Automator, and formed his power-pop band **Head Automatica** (along with then-fellow Glassjaw drummer Larry Gorman). At the same time, other 'Jaw alumni went on to play in bands like **Men, Women & Children** and **Classic Case**, neither of which made as much of an impact on the LI scene as Glassjaw. However, when Palumbo & Co. took a break, it allowed their peers to climb up the ranks and garner a shit-ton of national attention.

Music critics really started to focus in on Long Island after **Taking Back Sunday** and **Brand New** released their debut albums and earned a loyal underground fan base by tirelessly touring around the country playing anthemic songs off *Tell All Your Friends* and *Your Favorite Weapon*, respectively. Both bands' frontmen were enigmatic, boisterous, and untamed on stage, and it was only a matter of time before they duked it out for the title of Long Island Scene King. However, the real drama unfolded when a feud developed between the two bands after core members and former besties Jesse Lacey (from Brand New) and TBS then-guitarist John Nolan were torn apart by a spat of alleged girl-stealing and all-around ass-holery.[*] In turn, each group lashed out at the other in song (as heard on Brand New's "Seventy Times Seven" and TBS' "There's No 'I' In Team") and on merch (Brand New sold tees saying "Because Mics Are for Singing, Not Swinging," which was a blatant stab at frontman Adam Lazzara's[†] stage theatrics, while TBS offered up a cotton comeback with shirts that boasted "Proudly Swinging Since 1999"). Hatchets were eventually buried after Nolan (along with TBS bassist Shaun Cooper) left Taking Back Sunday to form **Straylight Run** and Lacey started writing about more pressing topics, like *Amélie* and Jesus Christ.

Sure, Lazzara's and Lacey's dreamy looks and introspective lyrics contributed to them quickly becoming poster children for the Long Island scene, but neither frontman would've made it out of playing

---

[*] *n.* Term to describe unscrupulous and unpleasant behavior of two assholes.

[†] Technically speaking, Adam Lazzara was born in Sheffield, Alabama, and spent most of his youth in North Carolina, but when the teenage troublemaker moved to Long Island in the late-'90s, he was quickly adopted by the scene and was always treated like one of their own. He also delivered Chinese food in a beat-up Honda. Way to keep it real, bro!

Centereach VFW Hall if not for **the Movielife**. Together from 1997 to 2003, the band earned a spot in the Long Island Hall of Fame by blending together pop-punk melodies (i.e., "Hey") with hardcore-inspired breakdowns (i.e., "Walking on Glass"), a sound that tough-guy bands from the 516 area code hadn't yet heard before. It was this signature sound that attracted Drive-Thru Records—a label brimming with

pop-punk powerhouses like New Found Glory and the Starting Line—which released two albums by the Movielife (2001's *Has a Gambling Problem* EP and 2003's *Forty Hour Train Back to Penn*) before the band hit the skids and decided to break up. Lead singer Vinnie Caruana went on to form **I Am the Avalanche**, a punk-infused indie band, while guitarist Brandon Reilly started the '80s-throwback **Nightmare of You**. Rumors of a Movielife reunion swirled in 2008, but the closest fans got to seeing the band happened at New Jersey's Bamboozle Festival when Caruana performed Movielife songs with a bunch of high school biology dweebs. (Oh, silly me. That was **Set Your Goals**. My bad.)

The Movielife's musical influence might not be immediately heard in the next generation of Long Island bands, but the group's lineage can definitely be traced to newcomers **This Is Hell**, which is carrying on the Strong Island hardcore torch thanks to the vocal styling of Travis Reilly, lil' bro of none other than Brandon Reilly. As for the rest of the scene's new batch of bands, they're nothing if not diverse: **Envy on the Coast** is pushing the envelope of post-hardcore by getting in touch with its alt-rock roots, as heard on their 2007 debut *Lucy Gray*. **As Tall**

as Lions is playing the type of dreamy and ambient indie rock not often associated with the overcast conditions of the East Coast. With its unique brand of fast, loud, and melodic punk, **Crime in Stereo** has earned comparisons to Gorilla Biscuits and has toured with everyone from Against Me! to Comeback Kid. On the other hand, **Bomb the Music Industry!** defy comparisons by embracing 23/4 time signatures, nearly twenty members, and a musical attitude that falls somewhere between ska, rock, and folk punk. Finally, there's **the Sleeping**, a post-hardcore powerhouse that was picked up by Victory Records in 2004 and caused jaws to drop four years later at 2008's Bamboozle Festival when it performed with Skid Row's Sebastian Bach. (Looks like that totally awesome supergroup VH1 formed for him didn't exactly work out, now, did it?)

STRONG ISLAND HARDCORE

The Long Island music scene wouldn't be what it is today without the founding fathers of yesterday—and those founding fathers kicked ass and took names. Sure, you already knew that Justin Beck was the guitarist of Glassjaw and owner of MerchDirect;* but did you know that before his tenure in the 'Jaw, he was playing in a Jewish straight-edge metalcore band called Sons of Abraham? Yeah, I didn't think so. Allow me to provide the following cheat sheet so you won't look like a total poseur next time you're in town.

MIND OVER MATTER

This Long Island quintet made waves in the scene when it took the standard hardcore formula created by legends like Gorilla Biscuits and Burn, and added an element of prog instrumentation and tex-

---

* Started by Justin Beck and friend Lee Tepper in 1999, MerchDirect is a full-service merch design, production, and distribution service for artists, musicians, and record labels. Clients include My Chemical Romance, Bleeding Star Clothing, and Perez Hilton.

LONG ISLAND

tured melodies never heard before. Many post-hardcore purists insist that without Mind over Matter, there would be no Glassjaw or Thursday, whose members, not surprisingly, could often be found in the pit at most MOM basement shows.

ESSENTIAL ALBUM: *Automanipulation* (**WRECKAGE, 1995**)

SILENT MAJORITY

It was embracing non-hardcore musical elements that really separated Silent Majority from the rest of its hardcore brethren, especially when crowds were more interested in heavy moshes, not heavy melodies. Never one to follow the pack, Silent Majority penned lyrics filled with rich images (as heard on songs like "Polar Bear Club" and "Arthur Trevor") and took musical risks by incorporating catchy melodies and complex rhythms into its unique sound (like on "Popular Opinion," which also features guest vocals by Daryl Palumbo). The band's impact on the hardcore landscape can be heard today in bands like Crime in Stereo and Capital, the newest outfit by Silent Majority vocalist Tommy Corrigan.

ESSENTIAL ALBUM: *Life of a Spectator* (**EXIT, 1997**)

SONS OF ABRAHAM

Sons of Abraham wasn't around for that long (two years, to be exact), but its imprint on the Long Island hardcore scene is still felt today. The band started out as a joke about being the world's first Jewish straight-edge band, but eventually turned into one of the first full-fledged metalcore acts. Guitarists Justin Beck and Todd Weinstock would eventually cause SOA to disband in 1998, when they would decide to join Glassjaw. It was then that vocalist Neil Rubenstein turned his attention to the business side of the scene by tour managing and working at LI's famed Downtown club before concentrating on his comedy career and life-long dream of being a poker dealer on Spike TV's *Casino Cinema*.

ESSENTIAL ALBUM: *Termites in His Smile* (**EXIT, 1997**)

CLOCKWISE

Before joining Taking Back Sunday, guitarist Eddie Reyes logged miles with a couple different Long Island groups, including this pre-emo, post-hardcore band. Originally known as No Thought, Clockwise would be known in Long Island's inner circle as *the* band that truly perfected the up-and-coming genre called emotional hardcore. Reyes teamed up with "General" George Fullan (who now engineers music for bands like the Color Fred, Kill Your Idols, and, *uh*, Cyndi Lauper) to form this Quicksand-inspired group, and this is where the axeman perfected the often-imitated Reyes Riff before joining the Movielife.
ESSENTIAL ALBUM: *Demos* (**SELF-RELEASED**)

VISION OF DISORDER

Though Vision of Disorder was often lumped into the Long Island hard-core scene, the band's music was heavily infused with elements of thrash and metal. The quintet managed to gain some mainstream attention when it released its second album on Roadrunner Records, *Imprint*, but

LONG ISLAND

never broke through to Middle America with its early attempt at what would later be called metalcore. The band eventually broke up in 2002, but vocalist Tim Williams and guitarist Mike Kennedy went on to form the shitty alt-metal act Bloodsimple, which can often be seen opening for shittier alt-metal bands like Stone Sour and Disturbed. Howev, fans who missed seeing Vision of Disorder the first time around can still re-live all the fist-pumping action by catching its performance in *N.Y.H.C.*, a documentary about, *duh*, the New York hardcore scene.

ESSENTIAL ALBUM: *Still* EP **(STRIVING FOR TOGETHERNESS, 1995)**

MUCHACHO MALO

That translates to "bad boy" (for all my non-Spanish-speaking readers), and Long Island has a ton of 'em, because if there's one thing that defines the area's hardcore scene, it's a certain sense of machismo. Here, I dissect the different ways that hardcore and post-hardcore types have achieved their much sought-after level of manliness, even while making some of the wimpiest music around. Read and learn.

GET A LOT OF TATTOOS

Nothing proves your manhood more than sitting for hours at a time in an oftentimes uncomfortable chair while some guy (or gal) with an extraocular implant* uses an electric machine to repeatedly drive a group of needles in and out of your skin at the speed of 80 to 120 times per second. Suggested designs include the Black Flag logo, the New York hardcore NYHC logo, or any piece of Derek Hess† artwork.

---

* Otherwise known as "eyeball jewelry" or "JewelEye," this procedure is currently untested outside of the Netherlands. However, if you hoof it overseas, for a mere 750 euros (that's almost twelve hundred dollars, depending on the exchange rate), you can have one of the following shapes implanted on your eyeball: heart, star, Euro-sign, four-leaf clover, or music note. Finally, my prayers have been answered!

† Cleveland-based poster artist whose scribble-style, low-brow art has also graced album covers by In Flames, Coheed and Cambria, and Clutch.

<125>

SPREAD YOUR SEED

If you really want to be a man, then you need to date a lot of chicks—and when I say "date a lot of chicks," I really mean "have a lot of sex with random girls you'll probably never call again." Morals and ethics don't really apply to men of the Long Island scene. (Which is weird because most of them have super-religious upbringings and are total mama's boys.) Forget about Jesus and your mother, pansy. It's scientifically proven that the more chicks you bang, the manlier you are.* Plus, be sure to use words like "bang," "pin," and "nail" when describing your sexual conquests. That'll definitely show your toolbag friends that you have no shred of sensitivity, in case they were unsure.

STOP EATING

No girl in her right mind likes a doughy dude. That's just a fact. So if you wanna be a real man, you better start by dropping some L-Bs. However, don't even think about doing it through a healthy diet coupled with a regular exercise routine. That kind of weight loss is for pussies—and guys who watch the Lifetime series *Army Wives*. I recommend sticking to a strict intake of cigarettes, Red Bull, black coffee, hard liquor, and the occasional slice of Umberto's pizza. Plus, a steady diet of nicotine, caffeine, and grease will help you achieve the final step of increasing your Long Island machismo, which is . . .

---

* It is not scientifically proven that being sexually promiscuous makes you a manlier man. However, it is true that being sexually promiscuous gives you a better chance of having a painful venereal disease, and if that won't put some well-needed hair on your chest, then I don't know what will.

LONG ISLAND

<126>

BE A DICK

To say that dudes in the Long Island scene have bad reputations is kind of like saying that human blow-up doll Heidi Montag *sorta* sings off-key. If you really wanna hang in the Long Island scene, then you have to be a tough-guy douchebag. Talk really loud at all times, pick fights for no reason, spill your drink on innocent bystanders, and then blame it on them. Just make sure to never apologize for anything. After all, being from Long Island means never having to say you're sorry.

CRY ME A RIVER

Unfortunately, Long Island will always be treated like the redheaded stepchild to the much hipper, cooler, and metropolitan New York City. Yes, residents can zip from Great Neck to Penn Station in nearly thirty minutes, but these two cities will forever remain worlds apart. It's enough to make anyone mad, especially if your Manhattan-based girlfriend just dumped you because she's tired of the commute and would rather date someone in Five O'Clock Heroes because he's, like, local and stuff.

It's because of this pain and suffering that the Long Island scene spawned some of the most beloved emo lyricists of the past decade. One listen to their lyrics and it's obvious these songwriters have serious issues to work through. In order to save them a trip to the psychiatrist, I've decided to diagnose them myself. You can thank me later, guys.

JOHN NOLAN FROM STRAYLIGHT RUN

DIAGNOSIS: Avoidant personality disorder
SYMPTOMS: Extreme shyness in social situations, highly self-conscious and self-critical, lonely self-perception, mistrust of others
SAMPLE LYRICS: "I'm listening to what they say / Feeling less and less okay" (from "How Do I Fix My Head" off *The Needles the Space*)

"A strong distaste for confrontation / Leaves no room for self expression / Such a strain to remain so docile / Though don't you know it all takes its toll" (from "It Never Gets Easier" off *Prepare to Be Wrong* EP)

"The words we say / Take different shapes / And you can only do so much / To try and get your point across" (from "The Words We Say" off *The Needles the Space*)

TREATMENT: Unless John participates in social-skills training, he's doomed to a life where he makes people feel awkward at parties—especially when they're stuck in a corner with him while he avoids eye contact and mumbles softly about his favorite Dave Eggers novel.

JESSE LACEY FROM BRAND NEW
DIAGNOSIS: Narcissistic personality disorder
SYMPTOMS: Inflated sense of self, erotic pleasure derived from contemplation or admiration of one's own body, lack of empathy for others
SAMPLE LYRICS: "Goodbye to love / Well, it's all right I'll push you right against the wall / Take apart your head right against the wall / Chew it up and swallow it" (from "Degausser" off *The Devil and God Are Raging Inside of Me*)

"Oh, I would kill for the Atlantic but I'm paid to make girls panic while I sing" (from "I Will Play My Game Underneath the Spin Light" off *Deja Entendu*)

"I used to pray like God was listening / I used to make my parents proud / I was the glue that kept my friends together / Now they don't talk and we don't go out" (from "Millstone" off *The Devil and God Are Raging Inside Me*)

TREATMENT: Because narcissism is considered to be an ingrained personality trait, there's no known medical treatment. *Great.* Guess the only thing to do is hide your mirrors and run away from Jesse "Enough About Me . . . More About Me" Lacey at the first mention of the ninth letter* of the alphabet.

---

* For anyone who can't count (or spell), that would be the letter *I*.

ADAM LAZZARA FROM TAKING BACK SUNDAY

DIAGNOSIS: Decidophobia*

SYMPTOMS: Fear of making bad decisions, excessive sweating, shaking, inability to think or speak clearly, fear of losing control, feeling of detachment from reality

SAMPLE LYRICS: "And I'm not so sure / If I'm sure of anything anymore" (from "The Blue Channel" off *Tell All Your Friends*)

"I always know how to avoid the issue / Got me alone so I couldn't address you" (from "The Union" off *Where You Want to Be*)

"So stop me if you've heard this one before / Sideways blinders / I can't find a way (around a way) around" (from "Miami" off *Louder Now*)

TREATMENT: Unless Adam participates in hypnotherapy, he's liable to find himself stuck in a sticky situation—like putting down the bottle, getting engaged to a religious female songstress, and moving to podunk Tyler, Texas, only to change his mind soon thereafter by

---

* Yes, this is totally a real disorder. Don't believe me? Wiki that shit!

breaking off his engagement, hitting the bars again, marrying a female bartender, and fathering a child. Come to think of it, I might be a little too late on this one.

DARYL PALUMBO FROM GLASSJAW/HEAD AUTOMATICA
DIAGNOSIS: Antisocial personality disorder
SYMPTOMS: Persistent lying, substance abuse, aggressive behavior, superficial charm, sense of extreme entitlement, bed-wetting
SAMPLE LYRICS: "(I'll hold) My child's head underwater / If it's a boy, I was joking / If it's a daughter, I'll say I did what I did because I had to . . . / And If you find my kid later, tell her I laughed, too" (from "Hurting and Shoving" off *Everything You Ever Wanted to Know About Silence*)

"I am the razor in the hands of your heart / And I am the razor in the hands of God" (from "The Razor" off *Decadance*)

"Loving you / If I can't have you, no one will / Love you / And for your love, I would kill" (from "Power Tool" off *The Impossible Shot* demos)
TREATMENT: Judging from the symptoms above, it's no wonder people suffering from antisocial personality disorder are often referred to as sociopaths. In the case of Daryl Palumbo, psychotherapy couldn't hurt—neither could Tranquility All-Through-The-Night briefs for the occasional bout of incontinence.

MAPPING OUT LONG ISLAND

CHILI'S GRILL & BAR (4100 HEMPSTEAD TURNPIKE, BETHPAGE, NY 11714; HTTP://WWW.CHILIS.COM)
Despite popular belief, not all Chili's are created equal—especially if you live in Long Island and pray at the altar of Jesse Lacey. Back in the day, Brand New practically lived in the vinyl booths here and was even rumored to take meetings with record label execs there when the quartet was looking to move from Triple Crown Records. Besides

LONG ISLAND

having really delectable Awesome Blossoms, this Chili's is a must-see because it was the site of a rather infamous fan appreciation party Brand New threw for the band's street teamers to celebrate the release of 2003's *Deja Entendu*. With any luck, you can still see footage of the fajita-filled soiree on YouTube.

THE ANGLE (267 MINEOLA BLVD., MINEOLA, NY 11501)

The Angle might not be around anymore, but it was one of the many places Artie Philie, aka "the godfather of Long Island," booked shows in the early '90s. Aside from renting the PWAC (People with Aids Coalition), Philie turned an otherwise cheesy dance club into a total hardcore hotspot. The venue closed in 1994, reopened three years later as Chunky's Bar and Dance Club, but eventually closed its doors for good in 2002. (C'mon, who wants to see shows at a place named after a dude called Chunky? Yeah, that's what I thought.) Philly, however, continues to be part of the scene by playing in local bands like Celebrity Murders.

LOONEY TUNES (31 BROOKVALE AVE., WEST BABYLON, NY 11704; HTTP://WWW.LOONEYTUNESCDS.COM)

In an age when mom-and-pop music stores are getting killed off faster than those castaways on *Lost*, this family-owned record store has been kicking ass and taking names for more than thirty years. That's not to say that Looney Tunes hasn't faced its share of obstacles—most recently in August 2007, when an electrical fire nearly scorched the whole lot. Thankfully, the Groeger brothers (who took over the business from their dad around 1992) were able to reopen the space nearly three months later, bigger and better than ever.

What makes Looney Tunes a beloved local favorite isn't just the store's unique and comprehensive inventory of CDs, DVDs, books, and random music memorabilia, but the venue's performance stage, which has hosted tons of in-store concerts from groups like Saosin and Circa Survive. Plus, Long Island bands—like Bayside and From Autumn to Ashes—always seem to make time to swing by, even if only for a short acoustic set or pizza party, and it's that local scene camara-derie that's helped this mom-and-pop shop outlast the rest.

EMPRESS DINER (2490 HEMPSTEAD TURNPIKE, EAST MEADOW, NY 11554)

Much like the Nautilis Diner in Massapequa, the Empress Diner is a postshow rest stop for anyone looking to regain some energy after a night of gnarly circle pits. This particular greasy spoon is a must be-cause it's open until 2:00 a.m. on weekdays and twenty-four hours on weekends. Plus, back in the day, it was a common hangout for the guys in Glassjaw. Who knows? With any luck you might still see members of Cardboard City stuffing their faces here.

AMF GARDEN CITY LANES (987 STEWARD AVE. #B, GARDEN CITY, NY 11530; HTTP://WWW.AMF.COM)

If there's one thing Long Islanders like just as much—if not more—than post-hardcore, it's bowling. Seriously. In addition to hosting Xtreme bowling parties and senior citizen leagues, this particular al-ley also hosted shows from bands like Silent Majority and Miracle of 86, acted as the headquarters of Fadeaway Records (responsible for putting out early records by the Movielife and Brand New), and em-ployed a certain Glassjaw guitarist by the name of Justin Beck. Natch!

PARKING LOTS

When you're a Long Island *yoot*,* the cityscape of New York City might look like it's a stone's throw away from Jackson Avenue, but Manhat-

---

* Also pronounced "youth," for those outside of Long Island.

tan's actually farther than you think—especially if you don't have a driver's license (or a MetroCard). Thank heavens for parking lots. Why, in the late '90s, there was a good chance you could find the future members of almost any Long Island hardcore or emo band biding their time in the cement corners outside the ol' Tower Records in Country Glen shopping center. You might not have a car to park, but you've definitely got a tush.

ROOSEVELT FIELD MALL (630 OLD COUNTRY RD., GARDEN CITY, NY 11530; HTTP://WWW.ROOSEVELTFIELD.COM)

When the fuzz has kicked you out of your parking lot sanctuary (see above), there's only one acceptable alternative: the mall. Roosevelt Field Mall, to be specific. You're bound to log some miles in a structure that harbors over 270 stores—not like you'd actually go in any. Except Urban Outfitters. . . . Or maybe Hot Topic. . . . And possibly H&M. . . . Hell, when you're bored, even Talbots can kill some time.

THE CRAZY DONKEY (1058 BROADHOLLOW RD., FARMINGDALE, NY 11735; HTTP://WWW .THECRAZYDONKEY .COM)

Along with venues like the Vibe Lounge, the Crazy Donkey is a relatively new addition to the Long Island scene. On nights when the club hosts shows, it attracts the likes of From Autumn to Ashes, Madball, and Cute Is What We Aim For, filling the void left by Farmingdale's now-defunct venue the Downtown. However, on the nights when the club hosts Jell-O wrestling, it attracts castoffs from A&E's *Growing Up Gotti*. Ouch.

A MOMENT OF SILENCE

THE DOWNTOWN (190 MAIN ST., FARMINGDALE, NY 11735)

The Downtown originally grew to prominence as a bar where you could catch cover bands like Kiss Me Deadly (an homage to Lita Ford) or Wizard of Ozz (an Ozzy Osbourne tribute band). The shows were twenty-one and up, and often started after 10:00 p.m. However, after many bands in the Long Island post-hardcore scene had outgrown their local VFW halls, someone had the brilliant idea to host Sunday matinee shows at the Downtown. Kids were stoked, money was made, and more shows were booked.

Soon after the success of these Sunday matinees, a guy named Adam Weiser (who now books all your favorite bands at the Starland Ballroom in Sayreville, New Jersey) snagged an assistant booking position and started bringing in up-and-coming bands like Motion City Soundtrack, the Ataris, and the All-American Rejects. Plus, not only could you catch an awesome set by Straylight Run, you could also toss back an order of mozzarella sticks and jalapeño poppers, thanks to a full kitchen that stood catty-corner to the stage. Unfortunately, infighting between the club's four owners eventually led to the venue's downfall and the Downtown officially closed its doors in 2005. There's always the Crazy Donkey, right?

September 16, 2001

On this night, local punk band the Influents is booked at 924 Gilman Street, a DIY punk venue in Berkeley, but the band cuts its set short so the members of Green Day can play an impromptu set—unbeknownst to fans and club volunteers. This marks the first time the trio has played the beloved club since becoming persona non grata after signing a major-label deal with Reprise Records in 1993. The trio hasn't played Gilman since, but its spontaneous performance can be seen in the Gilman with Green Day *DVD sold on the Influents' website.*

The Bay Area

Much to my surprise, the Bay Area is responsible for more than just launching a million Grateful Dead tribute bands. In fact, if not for this region of Northern California and its resident tastemakers, pop punk would never have hit the proverbial big time.

MUSIC PRIMER

For those of you who failed geography class, "the Bay Area" refers to the region of Northern California that encompasses big cities like San Francisco, San Jose, and Oakland. Known for its temperate climate and overall affluence, the Bay is also notorious for its huge population of hippies and homeless people—which, frankly, are kind of one and the same—who have occupied the area since the mid-'60s. That's when groups like the Grateful Dead, Big Brother and the Holding Company, and Jefferson Airplane ruled the scene. It was a simpler time back then. Love was free, acid was awesome, and people used things like daisies and raindrops for currency.

Peace was the order of the day, but it wouldn't be long until the scene got tired of deadbeats wearing tie-dye and the streets smelling like patchouli. The start of the Bay Area's post-hippie revolt really began with **Dead Kennedys**. Fronted by outspoken activist Jello Biafra, DK perfected the art of politi-punk, thanks in part to its debut *Fresh Fruit For Rotting Vegetables*, which contained "Holiday in Cambodia," a perfect example of the band's ability to capture po-

<138>

litical satire in song. Although the original lineup of DK parted ways in 1986, its legend continued to inspire a whole bunch of mouthy political bands who were always yammering on about some hot-button issue or another. The band eventually reformed in 2001 (with some creepy ex–child actor singing for Biafra), and Jello went on to become a sought-after spoken word artist and the spitting image of Boy George.

While Dead Kennedys was blowing minds for a living, **Operation Ivy** came on the scene and before long became ambassadors to the ska-punk movement, releasing two genre-bending albums in two years, 1988's *Hectic* and 1989's *Energy*. Though the band would break up the same month *Energy* was released, half the group—vocalist/guitarist Tim Armstrong and bassist Matt Freeman—would reform as **Rancid**, which along with **Green Day** and **NOFX** became the scene's forefathers of pop-punk. It was Rancid's straight-ahead approach to the burgeoning genre (as heard in songs like "Ruby Soho" and "Time Bomb" off 1995's . . . *And Out Come The Wolves*) that influenced other bands like **No Use for a Name** and **A Fire Inside** (known to fans as **AFI**).

Although it started off as a gritty hardcore band, over the years

AFI evolved into an MTV-approve, post-punk band with a flair for dramatics. However, back in the mid-'90s, when the group was busy getting Tim Burton tattoos and singing about death and destruction, the East Bay scene was brimming with indie excitement over groups like **Imperial Teen**, **Samiam**, **Mr. T Experience**, and a tough lil' band called **Jawbreaker**, which was led by the breathy vocals of Blake Schwarzenbach (who actually had throat surgery after releasing the trio's sophomore album, *Bivouac*). With so much momentum, many scenesters hoped Jawbreaker would make it big. Unfortunately, after its major-label debut, *Dear You*, failed to meet major-label expectations, the band split—though, oddly enough, the album that caused its demise would eventually become its masterpiece, according to new fans.

At the turn of the century, the Bay Area was ushering in a new crop of local scenesters who were all as diverse as the crowd at Fauxgirls!, San Fran's hottest drag cabaret. **Her Space Holiday** was a lean, mean remix machine—thanks to brain trust Marc Bianchi's indietronic touch on albums like *Manic Expressive*—in addition to mixing songs for Bright Eyes, R.E.M., and the American Analog Set. After somehow managing to get away from the drug-induced grip of Anton Newcomb and the Brian Jonestown Massacre, Peter Hayes started **Black Rebel Motorcycle Club**, a garage-rock revivalist trio that achieved minor success with blistering songs like "Whatever Happened to My Rock 'n' Roll (Punk Song)," which is one of the most underrated songs to spin at a hipster gathering. Yes, Bay Area music fans liked their rock hard, but they also liked it soft-boiled—hence the staggering-yet-perplexing success of VH1 mainstays like **Third Eye Blind** and **Counting Crows**.

As far as what the scene's like today, as long as 924 Gilman Street continues to thrive, there will always be a strong demand for punk and hardcore bands in the Bay. For example, **Tiger Army** has spent the past ten years pounding the pavement to become pomade-perfect kings of the psychobilly punk scene. **The Matches**, equally influenced by punk rock and vaudeville charm, have reinvented themselves more often than Madonna and, yet, have still managed to keep their fans along for the ride under the musical big top. Finally, bands like **Secondhand Serenade**, a tearjerker acoustic act centered around Menlo Park's John Vesely, and **Dance Gavin Dance**, a post-hardcore quintet on the rise, are bringing a lot of Warped Tour attention back to the scene. I'm not sure what former scene queen Janis Joplin would have to say about all the noise going on in the Bay Area nowadays, but that might be because she's, like, dead and stuff, which makes it kind of hard to talk.

LABEL CONSCIOUS

Like all good scenes, the Bay Area is home to two independent flagship labels that have released nearly all of the area's essential albums: First came **Lookout! Records**, which was started in Berkeley by Larry Livermore in 1987. The name originally came from *Lookout!* fanzine, which Livermore published until 1995, and from **the Lookouts**, a punk band Livermore put together with a then-unknown twelve-year-old neighborhood drummer named Frank Edwin Wright III, who soon earned the nickname Tre Cool. Lookout! Records eventually released numerous albums by the Lookouts, but the band went on indefinite hiatus when another local musician recruited Cool to play drums in his band. That local musician was Billie Joe Armstrong and his band was **Green Day**. Needless to say, the Bay Area music scene—and Lookout! Records—would never be the same.

Lookout! broke ground in the early '90s by releasing albums by **Operation Ivy**, **Crimpshrine**, **the Mr. T Experience**, **Blatz**, and a ton of other artists who frequented 924 Gilman, but the label really hit its stride after releasing Green Day's album *Kerplunk* (which then led to the band leaving Lookout! to sign with Reprise Records). Toward the end of the decade, Livermore turned over ownership of the label to Chris Appelgren, a longtime scenester who fronted local bands like **the PeeChees** and **the Pattern** and had worked at the company since its inception. Appelgren and Lookout! kept a finger on the pulse of un-

BILLY JOE MUST DIE

derground music by signing regional and national acts like **Ted Leo/ Pharmacists** and **the Donnas**, but the label soon fell into financial troubles, which was exacerbated in 2005 when Green Day rescinded its masters,* thus forcing Lookout! to lay off much of its staff and halt all new releases until the end of the year. Talk about some dookie.†

* Allegedly, Lookout! Records failed to compensate Green Day for money it earned from sales accumulated on its first two albums, *39/Smooth* and *Kerplunk*, which were released on the label before the band signed with Reprise. In turn, Green Day took back the master recordings from its first two albums or "rescinded its masters," leaving Lookout! unable to make future profits on them. Good for Green Day. . . . As for Lookout!, yeah, not so much.

† If that weren't enough, Operation Ivy did the same thing with its album *Energy*, which was then re-released on Hellcat in 2007. Damn, that's harsh.

In 1990, across the bridge in San Francisco, Mike Burkett, a slightly pudgy bassist, and his wife, Erin, started **Fat Wreck Chords**, a fiercely independent label, for his band **NOFX** and others like it to release their albums. Known for only offering one-record deals with bands whose members are over twenty-one, Fat Wreck has signed and released records by **Me First and the Gimme Gimmes**, **Propagandhi**, and **No Use for a Name**. Though many have gone on to sign deals with major labels (like **Rise Against**, **Against Me!**, and **Anti-Flag**), that hasn't stopped Fat Mike from expanding his Fat Wreck empire.

While the label continues to sign bands—like **Star Fucking Hipsters** and **Dead to Me**—Mike & Co. have set their sights on a variety of different media arenas. There's the world of publishing, in which Mike contributes to and distributes the quarterly mag *Punk Rock Confidential*; PunkVoter.com, Mike's coalition to unite, educate, and mobilize progressive voters for future elections; and, finally, there's the small screen, which he conquered by pitching, producing, and promoting *NOFX: Backstage Pass*, which was picked up by Fuse TV in 2007. Not for the faint of heart, *Backstage Pass* followed the inexplicable debauchery that trailed the pop-punk band during a 2007 tour, on which they hit far-flung locales from Peru to Japan. Throughout, the band incited a riot, snorted green cocaine, and made all sorts of smug private jokes—but, then again, would you expect any less from a group that released an album called *White Trash, Two Heebs and a Bean*?

ANATOMY OF A BAY AREA POP-PUNK BAND

Thanks in part to labels like Lookout! Records and Fat Wreck Chords setting up shop during the early '90s, the Bay Area soon became a breeding ground for pop-punk bands. Famous for bad homemade tattoos, Manic Panic–dyed hair, and singers in desperate need of an antihistamine, the pop-punk bands of yore (like NOFX and Samiam) would eventually inspire an entire musical movement.

In this section, let's break down the makeup of your typical Bay Area pop-punk band—and I'm not just talking about guyliner.

YOU'RE PART OF A BAY AREA POP-PUNK BAND IF YOU _____.

ALLOW ONE REALLY FAT, REALLY OLD, OR REALLY NERDY DUDE TO JOIN YOUR BAND

If we were to play the game One of These Things Is Not Like the Other and I show you a group shot of a typical Bay Area pop-punk band like Jawbreaker, you'd probably ask why Bill Gates was holding a bass. (Actually, that geeky-looking dude would be Chris Bauermeister, the band's bassist. *Duh.*) Needless to say, there's always one guy in the band who looks like he doesn't belong, and regardless of whether the one guy is fat, balding, ancient, or all three (as is the case with each of the members of NOFX), you can always count on Bay Area pop-punk bands to take pride in having a member who looks slightly like Dom DeLuise.

HASTILY DECIDE BAND NAME IN 30 SECONDS OR LESS

Let's just say that if you don't regret your band name for as long as your band was together, then you aren't truly part of the Bay Area pop-punk posse. How else would you explain monikers like Sewer Trout, the Skin Flutes, and Toiling Midgets?

WRITE LYRICS ABOUT HANGING OUT ON TRAIN TRACKS, DRINKING ON TRAIN TRACKS, OR SECURING FISHPLATES* TO TRAIN TRACKS

Okay, I made that last part up. Either way, Bay Area pop-punk bands seem to be inexplicably obsessed with train tracks for one reason or another. Perhaps it's because, much like rooftops and bridges (which

---

* *n.* Metal bar that is bolted down and connects two rails together on a track. Oddly enough, this has nothing to do with fish *or* plates. Weird, huh?

also provide a lot of inspiration for your average pop-punk scenester), railroad tracks are the perfect place to snag some alone time—*or* throw a raging bonfire with your gutter-punk pals from the slumburbs.* For some audio evidence of the tracks' significance, take a listen to Samiam's "While You Were Waiting" or Jawbreaker's "Condition Oakland."

DON'T CHANGE YOUR CLOTHES OR SHOWER. *EVER.*

Out on the West Coast, the worse you smell, the higher your street cred. In fact, the following whiff test can help match a person's stench to a person's cred:

> **Smells like:** Moldy sharp cheddar cheese
>   * **Level of cred: Introductory**
> **Smells like:** Rotten eggs marinated in dog urine
>   * **Level of cred: Intermediate**
> **Smells like:** Decomposing corpse soaked in baby vomit and ballpark mustard
>   * **Level of cred: Advanced**

If you ask me—or the members of Bay Area pop-punk bands who wear their body odor like a badge of honor—hygiene is so overrated.

PUT LITTLE TO ZERO THOUGHT INTO YOUR TATTOOS

Nothing screams "I'm in a Bay Area pop-punk band!" like a good ol' tat of a spiderweb around your elbow and the letters *P-U-N-X* spelled

---

* *n.* Suburbs that surround the outer edge of a city and are slowly inheriting the crime-infested living conditions often associated with the inner city. It would be as if *New Jack City* took place in abandoned McMansions.

out across your knuckles. Other acceptable designs include bike chain wheels, decapitated geishas, and Celtic ornamental bands. Brownie points if you gave yourself the tattoo—and managed to avoid contracting hepatitis C.

HOW TO LIVE ON THE CHEAP

Based on what you just learned, if you're giving yourself homemade tattoos, there's a good chance it's because you don't have a ton of cash burning a hole in your pocket. After all, thanks to those annoying Silicon Valley douchebags, San Francisco has slowly become one of the most expensive cities in the world. So what's a punk to do? Allow me to make a couple suggestions.

APPLY FOR FOOD STAMPS

Thankfully, scam punks* don't embarrass easily, thus they have absolutely *no* shame in working the system to their advantage. Their mantra might as well be "Damn the Man!" That said, being defiant can really work up an appetite, which is why food stamps are a godsend to punks who would rather starve than work at Starbucks. Silken tofu doesn't grow on trees, don't you know? Whether you're getting paid bumpkins at Aerators or are too lazy to stop playing Wii in your parents' basement, all you have to do is log on to the Food and Nutrition Service site (http://www.fns.usda.gov/fsp) to see if you are eligible for food stamps. Finally, a productive use for those stolen grocery carts you and your friends drunkenly ride in down Telegraph Avenue.

---

* *n.* A bunch of political-minded punks who are all about challenging the commercial establishment by conducting guerilla acts of rebellion against urban commerce. For more info, pick up *On the Lower Frequencies: A Secret History of the City* by Erick Lyle. . . . Or *don't*, because that's totally what the Man would want you to do.

THE BAY AREA

BE A FREEGAN

Freegans are the opposite of scam punks in that they are more interested in an anti-consumerist lifestyle that results in the limited consumption of resources. What does that mean, exactly? Freegans eat garbage. No, really. They give new meaning to the word "leftovers," considering most of their diet consists of what sustenance they find while Dumpster diving. Bin appetit!

COUCH SURF

Let me know if you've heard this one before: What do you call a musician without a girlfriend? The answer: Homeless. (Thanks, folks. I'll be here all night. Don't forget to tip your bartender.)

Not everyone can be multi-kazillionaires like Green Day, and because of this, I recommend the high art of couch surfing. Why pay a thousand dollars a month for a one-bedroom apartment in Berkeley when you can sleep on your friend's sketchy futon or half-full air mattress for *free*? The only downside to this method of housing is the possibility that your friends might get tired of your broke ass squatting in their living room and could potentially kick you to the curb. If that happens, I recommend you join the Couch Surfing Project (http://www.couchsurfing.com), which happily connects freeloaders to free accommodations all over the world.

BE A SPANGER

T-Boz from TLC isn't the only one who ain't too proud to beg, which is why you'll often see dirty punks begging for spare change all over the Bay Area. Sure, some of them might be homeless or destitute, but others might just be forty-five cents short of a chili verde quesadilla at Gordo on College Avenue.

SCAM KINKO'S TO PRINT YOUR FANZINE

Let's get something straight: I'm *not* an advocate of stealing for the sake of stealing. However, I *am* an advocate of stealing—er, being re-sourceful—for the sake of putting out a really killer fanzine. Making copies at your local Kinko's can be pretty pricey. With that in mind, I would innocently suggest using Kinko's lax black-and-white copy system to your advantage. When you tell a salesperson you want to make your own copies, you'll usually be given a card or a key to keep track of your paper use at the various self-service copy machines. Copy to your heart's content. Then, instead of turning in the card key and paying for your copies, simply walk out the door with the future issues of your literary masterpiece.* Lucky for you, print-shop employees are some of the most frazzled and befuddled human beings on the planet. Odds are, they'll be way too busy collating a massive document for the local bar association to notice you copying obscene amounts of *Up the Poop, Shoot.*†

---

* Warning: This maneuver is not for those often influenced by ethics, morals, or probation violations.

† Before you scour the Internet for back issues of *Up the Poop, Shoot*, I should probably tell you that I totally made this fanzine up. Don't hate. Congratulate.

HOOF IT TO THE HAIGHT

Speaking of people who look homeless, you can't visit the Bay Area without taking a trip to Haight-Ashbury. Once a bustling destination for peace, love, and hippie activity in the '60s, the Haight still remains a must-see for anyone looking to buy a new pair of devil sticks and wander around in a tie-dyed Steal Your Face T-shirt—or, more important, for anyone looking to point at, laugh at, and mock those buying a new pair of devil sticks and wandering around in a tie-dyed Steal Your Face T-shirt.

HEAD OVER TO A HEAD SHOP

Are you worried you might not pass your next drug test? Do you need to replace the glass water bong you accidentally dropped on the bathroom floor? Have you finally run out of penis enlargement pills? If you answered "yes" to any of the above (for reasons you don't need to explain to me, buddy), you have to visit these one-stop shops for barely legal and highly restricted goodness. Now if I could only remember which aisle that Volcano Vaporizer was in . . .

STOCK UP ON 420 PARAPHERNALIA

If you see someone wearing an article of clothing with the numbers "420" on it, there's a good chance that person loves to smoke the pot—and by "good chance," I mean, "you can bet your bottom dollar, Daddy Warbucks." Whether you want to get an authentic Wavy Gravy costume for next Halloween or buy pipe cleaner for your cousin who's a freshman at the University of Colorado at Boulder, you'll find no shortage of 420-enblazened paraphernalia on the Haight. Note to self: With so much to look at, there's a good chance you might lose track of time. In that case, try not to ask a stoner what time it is, because they'll probably say, giggling, "It's 4:20 somewhere in the world, *right*?" and then shove another handful of Cheetos in their mouth. Not helpful.

WHEN A LOCAL HIPPIE OFFERS YOU SOME "KILLER ACID," JUST SAY NO

This should be self-explanatory.

COUNT THE JERRY GARCIA LOOK-ALIKES

Grateful Dead tribute bands are a dime a dozen in the Bay Area, so it's no wonder that Haight-Ashbury is overflowing with paunchy, old Jerry Garcia look-alikes. With so much great eye candy, one of my fave pastimes is to play "Count the Jerrys" with my friends, and the first one to reach ten wins a cone of Ben & Jerry's Cherry Garcia ice cream from the store down the street. It's a win-win—especially considering you will have the munchies after getting a contact high just walking around this place.

JOIN A DRUM CIRCLE

Much as you do with cigarette butts, dirty pennies, and used condoms, you'll often find free-form drum circles littering the streets of the Haight. Whether beating on bongos or blowing a didgeridoo, these ragamuffins have one mantra—in addition to "metronomes are overrated"—and that's "the more, the merrier." So if you truly want to do as the locals do,

you'll grab a garbage can and start tapping. Musical aptitude not required; however, bonus points if you know the bass line to Bob Marley's "No Woman, No Cry."

BEWARE OF FALLING FOOTBAGS

Kicking a small beanbag with their feet is the extent of hippies' athletic ability and, thus, Hacky Sacking

THE BAY AREA

has become the unofficial sport of Haight-Ashbury. (Why else would the IFPA [International Footbag Players' Association] hold the Green Cup championships in Golden Gate Park every Memorial Day?) However, if you lack hand-eye coordination or aren't a fan of balls flying at your head, I'd recommend you watch your step because Hacky Sacks have been known to just drop out of people's patchwork pants without warning.

MAPPING OUT THE BAY AREA

BOTTOM OF THE HILL (1233 17TH ST., SAN FRANCISCO, CA 94107; HTTP://WWW.BOTTOMOFTHEHILL.COM)

Located in the once super sketchy Potrero Hill neighborhood of San Fran, Bottom of the Hill has been voted the city's *best* place to see live music by everyone from *Rolling Stone* to *Best of the Bay*. Tons upon tons of amazing acts (including the Donnas and One Man Army) have graced the stage here over the past fifteen years, inspiring an impressive array of posters and fliers from today's most cutting-edge contemporary artists, like Frank Kozik, Alan Forbes, and Coop. Check out the venue's website for a peak into its scrapbook.

THE GREAT WALL (6247 COLLEGE AVE., OAKLAND, CA 94618)

For veggie-friendly Chinese food, this is the place to go—especially if you're tired of fake meat that tastes like a wet sponge. Delectable dishes include the Great Wall's Mongolian beef, sesame chicken, and hot and sour soup, which is known to cure colds and clear sinuses. It's *that* powerful! Plus, any place that offers lunch for two for under fifteen dollars *and* a possible sighting of Billie Joe Armstrong is a must.

FAT SLICE (2375 TELEGRAPH AVE., BERKELEY, CA 94704; HTTP://WWW.FATSLICEPIZZA.COM)

This might not be your most health-conscious eatery, but Fat Slice always manages to hit the spot with obese pie portions, gooey cheese, and mile-high toppings. They also don't skimp on the grease, so make sure you pat your slice properly before you inhale or scope out the bathroom sitch to prepare for a possible ass-plosion. (Yeah, it goes there.) Also, before entering the establishment, gear up to battle the crowd of hungry homeless people who usually stand outside the entrance and beg you to buy them a slice. Sad but true.

924 GILMAN STREET (924 GILMAN ST., SAN FRANCISCO, CA 94146; HTTP://WWW.924GILMAN.ORG)

924 Gilman (or simply "Gilman," as the locals call it) is more than a just punk club; it's an institution. The all-ages, nonprofit venue opened in April 1986 to fill the void left after two of the city's most beloved clubs closed (see "A Moment Of Silence" below) and has remained one of the country's longest-running independent music venues ever since. Anyone who's been to Gilman knows it's a 100-percent DIY operation that has three steadfast rules: no drugs, no alcohol, and no violence— except for one unfortunate incident in 1994 involving Dead Kennedys' Jello Biafra, an aggressive slam dancer, and two broken legs.

Gilman also has a strict policy on racism, sexism, bigotry, and major-label artists: It won't stand for 'em. In addition to booking agents here requiring bands to submit lyrics before they are able to perform, the club also refuses to book bands that currently have major-label contracts. That means groups like Green Day, AFI, and Rancid—all of which grew up on this very stage—are now unwelcome here because of their current major-label record deals. (Not that Davey Havok & Co. are itching to play a two-hundred-person venue again, but that's besides the point. . . .) Despite all of its rules and regulations, though, Gilman remains a fave venue for fans and artists alike. After all, how many clubs offer concertgoers the opportunity to buy a two-dollar-per-year membership card that enables them to be directly involved in the club's constant improvement and decision-making process? Membership meetings are at 5:00 p.m. on the first and third Saturday of each month, so don't be late.

MILLENNIUM RESTAURANT (580 GEARY ST., SAN FRANCISCO, CA 94102; HTTP://WWW.MILLENNIUMRESTAURANT.COM)

Millennium is a far cry from the greasy goodness of Fat Slice, but it's equally as delicious—and less likely to clog an artery. Chef Eric Tucker, author of *The Artful Vegan*, has crafted the kind of hearty and healthy menu that satisfies both foodies and those who think Spam is a delicacy. However, you may want to bring your rich uncle with you, because the prices here don't exactly cater to spangers. Also, you might want to stash a food encyclopedia in your pocket, as well, to translate dishes like the semolina griddle cake, which is "brassica and collard green saag with tofu paneer, tamarind-red lentil sambar, spicy coconut chutney, and spring onion pakora." Say *what*?

KILOWATT (3160 16TH ST., SAN FRANCISCO, CA 94103; HTTP://WWW.BARBELL.COM/KILOWATT)

Back in the day, Kilowatt used to be the kind of place where bikers, punks, Goths, and seventeen-year-old high schoolers with fake IDs could unite and throw back a frosty cold one. Unfortunately, times have changed. The door guy actually checks IDs closely now and hipsters and yuppies have replaced most of the local outcasts. Still, I can't help but have a soft spot in my heart for this place, thanks to their cheap brews, dartboards, and dogs-welcome policy. After all, there's nothing better than getting hammered while a cockapoo sniffs your crotch.

STORK CLUB (2330 TELEGRAPH AVE., OAKLAND, CA 94612; HTTP://WWW.STORKCLUBOAKLAND.COM)

You don't have to venture across the Golden Gate Bridge to visit a great DIY dive bar: Enter Oakland's Stork Club, which is the perfect place to listen to a local death-metal band, watch Belles du Jour perform burlesque every Monday night, or just zone out and play pinball. One of the best things about this place? They book anyone. One of the worst things? They book *anyone*. Don't say I didn't warn you.

LUCKY 13 (2140 MARKET ST., SAN FRANCISCO, CA 94114)

Authentic rocker bars are hard to come by, which is why I'm totally thankful for Lucky 13. You totally can't beat this place's cheap (and stiff) drinks, photo booth, and non-elitist attitude. Come for the endless supply of free popcorn, stay for the Misfits song on the jukebox and $2.50 happy hour.

ROCK PAPER SCISSORS COLLECTIVE (2278 TELEGRAPH AVE., OAKLAND, CA 94612; HTTP://WWW.RPSCOLLECTIVE .COM)

I wish more scenes had projects like the volunteer-run Rock Paper Scissors Collective, which promotes and encourages local artists to share their creative vision with the community. Not only does RPS offer a retail space for artists to sell their handmade goods, but also, when you buy something from the store, 60 percent of your purchase goes directly to the artist while 40 percent goes back into keeping the doors at RPS open. Plus, the Collective offers a bevy of classes where

you can learn everything from "Beginning Book Binding" to "Under-wear Making." No artistic ability required but materials and class fees may vary.

THRILLHOUSE RECORDS (3422 MISSION ST., SAN FRAN-CISCO, CA 94110; HTTP://WWW.THRILLHOUSERECORDS.COM)

What was once known as Epicenter, a long-gone punk-rock record store where Jawbreaker's Blake Schwarzenbach blew much of his advance from Geffen, has given way to Thrillhouse Records, a not-for-profit, all-volunteer-run record store and label. There's always a party going on here, whether it's in the basement, behind the counter, or at the annual Thrillfest concert. Plus, the face-tattooed clerks are always willing to put on any album you want so you can hear it before you buy.

A MOMENT OF SILENCE

THE MABUHAY GARDENS (443 BROADWAY ST., SAN FRAN-CISCO, CA 94133)

In an area of San Fran that was best known for its overwhelming se-lection of strip clubs, the Mabuhay Gardens stood loud and proud as one of the city's lone punk venues. After booking everyone from the Avengers to Black Flag, Iggy Pop to Redd Kross, the Mab quickly became an important stop for national bands touring California, and it wasn't long until fans started to refer to it as "the West Coast CBGB." However, it was one infamous gig in January 1978 that propelled the club into punk-rock infamy: It was on this stage that the Sex Pistols played the last gig on their now-infamous American tour, which caused Johnny Rotten to quit and the other members to eventually disband. Not an easy feat for a former Filipino restaurant.

Unfortunately, the music scene changed over the years, key promoter/local radio personality Dirk Dirksen lost interest in emceeing the punk palace, and Mabuhay closed its doors for good in 1986. Sure, most of you probably weren't even conceived when the club rose to punk-rock prominence, but you can still relive the excitement in *Our Band Could Be Your Life: Scenes from the American Indie Underground 1981–1991*, required reading for anyone aspiring to be a true scenester. Oh, and if it makes a difference, Metallica played some of their earliest shows here. Yeah, I didn't think so, either.

October 9, 2001

A then-unknown, much-hyped band called the Strokes released its debut album, Is This It, *setting the stage for one of the most talked about rock scenes of the decade. Not only would this group of overprivileged private-school chums spark a musical revolution, but it would also inspire its peers to adopt a strict no-food diet, invest in multiple pairs of skin-tight Diesel jeans, and try to snag Hollywood arm-candy like Drew Barrymore and Amanda de Cadenet.*

New York, New York

It's safe to say that no other music scene in the world is more revered than the one in New York City. Yet, while the Big Apple has contributed to various genres in the underground musical landscape over the years, most recently it has spawned the kind of unfailingly hip rock bands that seem to exist solely on cigarettes and overpriced vodka tonics.

MUSIC PRIMER

Over the years, a lot has gone on in New York City, making it difficult to figure out what you should—and shouldn't—include when retelling this scene's musical history. Sure, I could talk about the folk soundscape of the 1960s, the classic-rock boom in the 1970s, or even the disco and hip-hop craze that took shape in the 1980s. However, for the purpose of this book, I'm going to narrow things down considerably by focusing on the part of the city's music scene that generated the kind of smug hipsters who act as if it's their job to smoke cigarettes and appear unimpressed by practically everything. You know the type.

These days, most people in NYC will agree that **the Velvet Underground** epitomized this blasé attitude. Formed in 1965 (long before singer Lou Reed began looking like a tan salamander), the Velvets were a co-ed rock collective that wrote songs about drug dealers, heroin, and drug dealers who sold heroin. They were the house band at Andy Warhol's art commune, the Factory, and really turned heads once they hooked up with Nico, a stone-faced German model with a monotone vocal range, and released songs like "I'm Waiting for the Man" and "Venus in Furs." Yet, while the Velvet Underground proved to be incredibly important to the hipster masses, it was only the first in the scene. Nearly a decade later, in 1977, a band called **Television**, which was lead by a gangly guy who looked like an eighth-grade geometry teacher, started making post-punk strides with its break-through album *Marquee Moon*. Unfortunately, the group's follow-up record wasn't as well received as its debut; this, coupled with infighting and rumors of drug abuse, led the quartet to disband in 1978, though it would reconnect two more times over the next twenty-five years. To their credit, music critics and musicians still cite *Marquee Moon* as an essential album and Television *did* play one of the first shows at CBGB, breaking ground for a whole bunch of adventurous bands that would spend the next few years not only playing there, but holding their noses while using the club's notoriously filthy bathroom.

Talking Heads, **Patti Smith**, and **Blondie** were also among the acts that called CBGB home in the late '70s. However, it was a leather-clad, delinquent foursome who would end up taking a residency at the Bowery venue and inadvertently creating a new musical genre—punk rock. Though it was more than thirty years ago, **the Ramones** wore all the same clothes as your average 2009 hipster (i.e., leather jackets, dirty denim, and worn-out Converse high-tops) and looked deadly cool doing so. Coincidence? I think not. Plus, instead of writing songs about psycho killers and glass hearts, like their art-rock peers, the Ramones concentrated on singing about the simpler things in life: sniffing glue, dancing the twist, and stealing your friend's girlfriend. Though they encountered more lineup changes than there are Jolie-Pitt children, the Ramones are largely credited with making punk palatable, which, unfortunately, marked the end of an era in New York City.

Mayor Rudy Giuliani was cleaning up the streets and not even the city's music scene was safe from his disinfectant wrath. Sure, there were some bands that came up during the '90s (such as **Helmet** and **the Jon Spencer Blues Explosion**) that geeky audiophiles would probably consider "revolutionary"; but when it comes to the kind of grimy rock bands that inspired fans to stay out way too late on a work night or go an entire week without showering, it wasn't until the end of the decade that things really got down and dirty again. Oddly enough, it would be five rich kids with hard-to-pronounce names who would end up capturing what it felt like to be drunk and walking around the East Village at four in the morning. For that reason, it seemed like **the Strokes** would be the kind of band only alcoholics living in the East Village would relate to, but that wasn't the case, because shortly after releasing their first record *Is This It*, the Strokes became big. Like, *really* big. So big that drummer Fabrizio Moretti started dating Drew Barrymore, Slash inexplicably appeared in their video for "Someday," and yes, they experienced the official rite of passage for any bloated, self-obsessed rock band—they hired bodyguards.

While Fab and the gang were busy hanging out with Cameron Diaz, other NYC upstarts were making headlines. For example, **the Yeah Yeah Yeahs** were on the forefront of the Williamsburg art-rock scene thanks to cacophonous feminist anthems like "Bang!" and lead singer Karen O, a schizophrenic style maven who wasn't afraid to wear a garbage bag as a cocktail dress. Then came **Interpol**, whose love for Joy Division was almost matched by its love for three-piece suits. In fact, each member was constantly dressed to the nines. Say you saw its singer Paul Banks at the corner deli? He was probably wearing a suit. Maybe you saw its guitarist Daniel Kessler walking his dog in Tompkins Square Park? Again, a suit. Perhaps its drummer Greg Drudy was working out at the 24 Hour Fitness in Chelsea? Yup, another suit. This is the kind of band Interpol was and, without question, its biggest star was bassist Carlos D, who inspired more online rumors than practi-

cally anyone else in New York at the time,* due in part to DJing† at hipster bars and clubs where nerdy white kids went to dance.

Now, that last line is not a typo: By the mid-2000s, many New Yorkers thought dance punk was going to be the Next Big Thing and, because of this, funky Brooklyn bands like **Radio 4** and **the Rapture** suddenly found themselves being flown around the world to play high-profile shows and DJ at the posh after-parties. So, did any of them ever make it big? Let's put it this way: Last I heard, the members of the Rapture were still DJing—at weddings and bat mitzvahs. After dance-punk failed to catch on, critics hoped anti-folk bands like **the Moldy Peaches** and **the Trachtenberg Family Sideshow Players** were going to take over the dial. Unfortunately, the mainstream music-buying public wasn't digging on songs about Long John Silver's and pooping your pants—that is, until Diablo Cody said it was okay.‡ (Go figure.) Finally, there was the whole electroclash movement, which was spearheaded by gay-tastic groups like **Fischerspooner**, **A.R.E. Weapons**, and **Scissor Sisters**. Elton John counted himself as a fan, but he was really the only one.

Yes, it was a sad state of affairs. By the decade's end, it seemed as if many New York City scenesters were so disheartened by the direction that things were heading, they decided to pack it in. The Strokes, for one, began having babies and God knows nothing can ruin a perfectly good outfit more than some punk-ass little kid throwing up all over it. It was rumored that the Yeah Yeah Yeahs were heading for splitsville after Karen O moved out to L.A. and started dating director Spike Jonze,

---

* This is no slight exaggeration. In the past few years, the rumors about Carlos D have included that he doesn't allow himself to be exposed to daylight, and that he is only attracted to overweight women with red hair.

† In New York City, people use the term "DJing" *very* loosely. Usually, this refers to bringing your iPod to a bar and playing the first Killers record while you high-five a bunch of drunk people. Now, *that's* entertainment.

‡ Movie fans fell in love with the Moldy Peaches song "Anyone Else but You" after it was featured in the ending scene of *Juno*. I wonder if fans also fell in love with the line, "Squinched up your face and did a dance / Shook a little turd out of the bottom of your pants."

though the trio insists they are indeed still together and are working on their third album. The members of Interpol, for the most part, also moved out of Lower Manhattan and, in the case of Carlos D, traded in the tailored suits for Western shirts and bolo ties.

This isn't exactly encouraging for anyone who is just discovering the New York City scene, but don't fret. While the current musical landscape may not feel as cool as it once did, you can be sure that a new generation of local hipsters will soon emerge.

THE ART OF DOWNTOWN COOL

Breaking through the inner echelon of New York City cool isn't something that happens overnight—or something you can figure out by reading a history that spans a few pages in a book like this, either. No, exhuming cool in NYC takes practice, which is why I have developed a step-by-step guide to help you out in social situations. Prepare to be very, very popular.

STEP 1: MAKE EVERY SIDEWALK A CATWALK

Every time you step out on the streets of New York City, you should be strutting your stuff like you're Naomi Campbell: You should be fierce, you should be fabulous, and most importantly, you should able to chuck your BlackBerry at an assistant standing fifty feet away. Because of this, a lot of thought and creativity should go into your ensemble before leaving your apartment. Whether you decide to wear an oversized Mickey Mouse glove on your head (à la MisShapes sidekick Sophia Lamar) or squeeze into a pair of gold lamé leggings (like any underage salesgirl at American Apparel), much of the New York scene's fashion aesthetic is based on a fake-it-'til-you-make-it mentality. That's why, with a little ingenuity, anything can be fashionable.

STEP 2: THE MORE HOMELESS YOU LOOK, THE MORE STYLISH YOU ARE

Not sure how to incorporate random items like a tube of Orajel and an empty pizza box into a cohesive outfit? Try to remember that less is more—and by "less," I mean "home-less." After all, how many times have you accidentally tossed a quarter into a bum's Styrofoam coffee cup only to realize that the bum was actually Julian Casablancas? (I

lost count, too.) Mary Kate Olsen may've popularized boho chic, but it's really hobo chic that's taking over the city. How else would you explain an aspiring bag lady like Chloë Sevigny getting her own clothing line for Opening Ceremony?

STEP 3: WHEN STANDING AGAINST A WALL, ALWAYS POSE

Now that you're looking cool, be prepared for those around you to want to capture your coolness on film. It's only natural, because you never know when the photographers from LastNightsParty* might be lurking around. When you're hailing a taxi? Pose. When you're ordering a drink? Pose. When you're using the urinal? Pose. If you must, practice in front of the bathroom mirror—or consult any image of Leigh Lezark. She ain't called Princess Coldstare for nothing.

STEP 4: IF YOU'RE EVER IN A SITUATION WHERE YOU DON'T KNOW ANYONE IN THE ROOM, BREAK OUT YOUR PHONE AND START TEXTING

Looking fierce can often be intimidating to others less cool, so don't be surprised if your clenched jaw and stoic gaze drives people away. Luckily, being social doesn't mean you actually have to interact with those around you. After all, that's what cell phones are for. Conversations are so much better experienced through texts and IMs. That way, you don't have to worry about things like awkward pauses, bad breath, or non-abbreviated sentences. Like I always say in the book of downtown cool, *looking* popular will ultimately *make* you popular.

STEP 5: SAYING YOU KNOW HOW TO DJ WILL ALWAYS BOOST YOUR CRED–REGARDLESS OF WHETHER YOU CAN ACTUALLY DJ OR NOT

Back in the day, when DJing was an art form, it was all about slip-

----

* Founded by musician/photographer Merlin Bronques in 2004, LastNightsParty .com is a website dedicated to the decadent debauchery of NYC nightlife. The site often features shots of overdressed partygoers at various soirees around the city or naked hipsters romping around in sparse studio apartments and public showers.

<167>

cueing, harmonic mixing, and beat matching. Today, it's more about pretending to slip-cue, mix harmonies, and beat-match when you're actually just pressing buttons on your iPod. Still not convinced? How do you think scenesters like James Iha, Pete Wentz, or any of the Madden brothers landed spinning gigs?

STEP 6: WHEN IN THE COMPANY OF SOMEONE FAMOUS, NEVER ACKNOWLEDGE THEM DIRECTLY

Instead, secretly take a picture of them on your camera phone and blog about it later. You'll be *much* better off for it.

THE ABCS OF NYC

Now that you've been given a cheat sheet to maneuver through NYC's labyrinth of social etiquette, you may think that you've learned everything you need in order to properly navigate the local scene. But think again. You see, in the city that never sleeps, there is no shortage of things one must learn in order to properly fit in, and there are all sorts of characteristics that continue to define the area. So how can you remember them all? Here are the ABCs of everything else you'll need . . .

A IS FOR ALPHABET CITY.

The New York City neighborhood between Avenue A and Avenue D is called "Alphabet City." However, despite the *Sesame Street*-sounding moniker, there's nothing innocent about this area. In fact, there was a time not so long ago when living in this particular Manhattan neighborhood meant you had a death wish. However, with housing prices on the rise, I don't know which I'm more afraid of here: my life savings being stolen by a scary mugger or a scarier real estate broker.

B IS FOR BRUNCH.

In New York, brunch serves as a serious indicator that your days as a hard-partying scenester are over. That's why your average New York

City scenester's heavy brunch-eating period will inevitably come shortly after a decision to move to Park Slope and replace the subscription to *Paste* with one for *The New Yorker*.

C IS FOR COCAINE.

Trying to find cocaine in Manhattan is like trying to find a contaminated needle in Amy Winehouse's flat; it's everywhere! Don't get me wrong. I totally know that drugs are bad and stuff. Howev, I can't help but be slightly impressed that you can get illegal substances delivered like Domino's Pizza in New York City.

D IS FOR DARKROOM.

Over the years, the Darkroom has served as a serious hipster hangout for scenesters on the Lower East Side. It has also been home to many firsts: The first time a Stroke was recognized in public, the first time Carlos D stepped out as a DJ, and the first time two of society's brightest minds, Lindsay Lohan and Kate Moss, partied together. Now *that's* history.

E IS FOR EXCREMENT.

It's a little known fact, but sadly there is more fecal matter lining the streets of New York than seemingly any other city in the Western world. Want to know what makes this particular statistic even worse? It's usually *human* excrement, which proves that your average homeless person in New York is eating more often than the hipsters here. Speaking of which . . .

F IS FOR FOOD.

Remember this stuff? Well, if you want to keep your status in the current New York City music scene, then you're going to have to kiss the concept of eating good-bye. After all, how are you supposed to fit into a ridiculously tiny pair of tapered black jeans if you do something stupid like *feed* yourself?

G IS FOR *GOSSIP GIRL.*

I'm not sure how accurate this depiction of Upper East Side private-school life is, but I really don't care. This show is more addictive than crack. So what if Serena van der Woodsen killed a guy in a botched sex tape or if Blair Waldorf's Valentino Couture Braided Tote costs three times as much as my rent? It's those kind of ridiculous plotlines and unrealistic financial expectations that make me love this series even more.

H IS FOR HAMPTONS.

Yes, I'm talking about the same Hamptons where P. Diddy chills with Martha Stewart at his famous white parties. What does this stuffy, Long Island neighborhood have to do with the scene happening in Manhattan? Not a whole lot. It's just that while you're slumming it on the Lower East Side, the incredibly good-looking author of this book will be popping Cristal at Denise Rich's annual garden party.

I IS FOR ITCHING.

This is fairly common symptom that you may begin to develop after spending a bit too much time in bars on the Lower East Side. In fact, it may really start to flare up if you are the type of guy or girl who is prone to hooking up with a total stranger in the bathroom. Seriously, if this occurs repeatedly, don't be proud. Just take your ass to the free clinic.

J IS FOR JULIA ALLISON.

For anyone living under a digital rock for the last couple years, Julia Allison is the newly crowned queen of online self-promotion. (No, seriously. *Wired* featured her on the cover for that very reason.) Move over, ForBiddeN. Do another lame gender-confused dating show, Tila Tequila. Allison's brand is all the rage, as exhibited by the show she developed for Bravo called *IT Girls*. (That's "IT" as in "Information Technology." Punny, huh?) No matter how much you hate her—whether it be for the inane vignettes about her Shih Tzu sitting on conveyor-belt checkouts or her ridiculous lip-dubs to "A Whole New World" from *Aladdin*—if you call yourself a true NYC scenester, you're definitely going to tune in, even if it's just to post nasty comments on Gawker.

K IS FOR *KIDS.*

When it was originally released in 1995, this Larry Clark–directed, Harmony Korine–penned drama was hugely controversial for its supposed real-life depiction of teen life in New York City. Clark and Korine used unknown or first-time actors—like Rosario Dawson, Chloë Sevigny, and Leo Fitzpatrick—who were all super young, which made watching them simulate having sex, doing drugs, and getting into fights all the more disturbing. Even the mere thought of it now makes my stomach turn. *Shudder.*

L IS FOR L TRAIN.

This train line takes New Yorkers from the heart of Williamsburg to anywhere along the northern tip of Lower Manhattan. It's also the most unreliable goddamn subway line in the world. Seriously, if you have not punched a wall out of frustration waiting for this thing, well, give it a couple weeks. You will. And when you do, know that you are *that* much closer to becoming a tried-and-true NYC scenester.

M IS FOR MisSHAPES.

Ah, MisShapes. Is it a party? Is it a person? Is it a place? Actually, it's all three—sort of. Named after a Pulp song, MisShapes was a weekly Saturday night party originally held at the West Village bar Luke & Leroy's and later at a skeezy bar called Don Hill's. The night was hosted by the gorgeously emaciated triple threat of Geordon Nicol, Leigh Lezark, and Greg Krelenstein, who first met at a Tiswas bash in 2001. Three years later, the trio—dubbed collectively as "The MisShapes"— took over the Downtown scene with its weekly soiree, which started attracting the likes of Madonna and Pulp's own Jarvis Cocker.

For all the love media outlets like *Teen Vogue* and *Paper* magazine gave the 'Shapes, there were some definite haters (like those at

Gawker who lovingly referred to Nicol as "Leotard Fantastic," Lezark as "Princess Coldstare," and Krelenstein as, well, "The Other Guy"). No matter. Nothing could stop the three otherwise insignificant NYC scenesters—who, we'll admit, happened to have amazingly good bone structure—from becoming a national sensation.

Sadly, the weekly party officially closed its doors in September 2007, but the majesty of MisShapes lives on. There's *MisShapes*, the book; MisShapes, the runway models; MisShapes, the DJ team; Mis-Shapes, the clothing line; MisShapes, the no-annual-fee credit card; MisShapes, the instant stain remover; and MisShapes, the ultra-thin regular maxi-pad with wings. Okay, I'm only kidding about those last couple, but, hell, I wouldn't be surprised if that crap popped up eventually . . .

N IS FOR NEW JERSEY.

Despite the fact that many NYC transplants were actually born and raised in the beloved Armpit of America (aka New Jersey), you'd be hard-pressed to find anyone who would willingly admit it. How come? Well, I can't think of anyone who would want to brag about growing up in an armpit. Can you?

O IS FOR OPEN BAR.

What's an open bar? (Oh, that's cute.) It's another long-standing tradition that most New Yorkers are all too familiar with. How does it work? You show up to a bar at a certain time, and thanks to a local sponsor, the drinks are free. Yup, totally gratis. With so many scenesters New York City paying eighteen hundred dollars for a one-room studio apartment, it's no wonder they worship this concept.

P IS FOR PARK SLOPE.

As I previously mentioned, there will definitely comes a time in scenesters' lives when they have to admit they are getting old. And by "old," I mean they're turning thirty. When that happens, well, there is only one place that they will head: Park Slope, a somewhat quiet Brooklyn neighborhood where everyone has a passing knowledge of pricey microbrews and, worse yet, actually enjoys watching reruns of *King of Queens*. I know. It's a scary thought. But so is getting old.

Q IS FOR QUEENS.

For the most part, there's really no reason to go to Queens—unless you're looking to get held up at knifepoint. Then, by all means, go ahead.

R IS FOR REHAB.

Okay, maybe not all NYC scenesters are in need of a trip to see Dr. Drew (you know, the oddly attractive white-haired dude from VH1's *Celebrity Rehab*), but if you are hanging out with the kind of locals who are constantly wiping their nose after going to the bathroom every ten minutes, there's a slight chance that they might be heading for an all-expense paid, sixty-day getaway. If this happens to any of your friends, don't despair. Maybe they can get you an autograph from Lindsay Lohan.

S IS FOR SEVIGNY.

When you're living in New York, you are bound to see a couple of celebrities running around. But no one is more ubiquitous in Lower Manhattan than Chloë Sevigny. One day she'll be traipsing out of Happy Ending on the Lower East Side. The next she'll be eating a taco at the San Loco on Rivington. And the day after that, if you're really lucky, you'll see her buying impetigo ointment at the K-Mart on Astor Place. Whatever the case, if you hang around NYC long enough, you will definitely run into the *Big Love* star—just make sure you don't get too close, especially if she has impetigo.

T IS FOR "THE."

There are more bands with names that start with the word "the" per capita in New York City than practically any other city in the U.S. For further proof, check out the Strokes, the Rapture, the Bravery, and, well, the Band That Just Started Five Minutes Ago While You Were Reading This Book.

U IS FOR ULTRAGRRRL.

In any other city, Sarah "Ultragrrrl" Lewitinn would probably be considered just another hyperactive Jewish girl who loves U.K. rock bands a bit too much for her own good. But in New York City, she is both an undeniable scene fixture and an ever-present DJ who gets hired by practically every promoter in Manhattan. That being said, any newcomer to the scene should be prepared to hear her play "Love Will Tear Us Apart" roughly three million times at your local bar. Seriously.

V IS FOR VICENT GALLO.

To most of the world, Vincent Gallo is known as the short-tempered director/actor of such films as *Buffalo 66* and *The Brown Bunny*. But to many young girls in Lower Manhattan, Gallo is better known as the old dude that's constantly hitting on you by bragging about directing and acting in *Buffalo 66* and *The Brown Bunny*. So the next time you're walking through SoHo wearing hot pants and you hear a catcall, chances are it won't be an overweight construction worker who's yelling at you. It'll be this middle-aged dude.

W IS FOR WINDSOR KNOT.

Unless you worked at a bank in high school, you may need to learn how to tie this knot. After all, most self-respecting scenesters here have long since mastered this technique to help accent their outfits. If this particular method is new to you, here's what you'll need to know: First, hang the tie twelve inches below your chest. Then, cross over the tie's blunt end to the right-hand side and then . . . Oh, for Christ's sake, just go ask your dad.

X IS FOR X-RAY.

As in, "I totally fell down the stairs at this bar last night and I had to get an X-ray. Now I can't pay next month's rent." Sucks to be you.

Y IS FOR "YOU'VE NEVER HEARD OF THEM?"

This sentence is something your average know-it-all New York City scenester will say about three thousand times on any given night. Usually, they will do so when discussing the obscure indie band that they saw the night before at Mercury Lounge. "Dude," they will often begin, "I totally saw the Radioactive Testes last night and it was awesome. What, you've never heard of the Radioactive Testes? Where have *you* been?" This particular dialogue will then be followed by said scenester rolling his or her eyes at you. When this occurs, if at all possible, try to refrain from immediately strangling the person.

Z IS FOR ZZZZ.

Generally speaking, "zzzz" is the sound you make when you're sleeping. You remember sleep, right? Well, along with eating and having money in your checking account, this is *definitely* something you will have to kiss good-bye in order to survive in New York City.

<176>

MAPPING OUT NEW YORK CITY

BLACK AND WHITE (86 E 10TH ST., NEW YORK, NY 10003)

Located in the heart of the East Village, Black and White is the kind of bar where you can find Kelly Osbourne sucking face with some eighteen-year-old baby-faced male model on the front steps while the former frontman of From Autumn to Ashes buses tables inside. (Oh, how the mighty have fallen. Wait . . . FATA were hardly considered mighty. Nevermind.) Before NYC adopted a nonsmoking policy, barhoppers could barely see two steps in front of them, let alone the gin and tonic they just ordered. However, now that the nicotine cloud has lifted, you can see the drinks—and the patrons—perfectly, which isn't necessarily a good thing if you happen to be sitting next to any of the members of Mooney Suzuki.

BOWERY BALLROOM (6 DELANCEY ST., NEW YORK, NY 10002; HTTP://WWW.BOWERYBALLROOM.COM)

Nothing suggests that you've made it in the New York City scene more than playing a show at this cavernous rock club. Back in the day, the Strokes packed out the Bowery, and so did Interpol and the Yeah Yeah Yeahs, all right before they became famous. Today, that pattern continues, and because of this, there's usually no better way to tell that a band destined for greatness than by its playing a sold-out show here.

CBGB (315 BOWERY, NEW YORK, NY 10003; HTTP://WWW .CBGB.COM)

Founded in 1973 by Hilly Kristal, CBGB hosted pretty much every punk band on the planet during the club's thirty years on the Bowery. While booking a show at CB may have been a rite of passage, I can think of a couple reasons why bands may've hated playing here: (1) It was a shit-hole, (2) the manager was a dick, (3) the entire place smelled like urine, and (4) did I mention the place was a shit-hole? Before Kristal died in August 2007, it was said that he planned to reopen the dive in Las Vegas, while the Bowery location reopened as a John Varvatos clothing store.

Did you hear that? It was Joey Ramone turning over in his really long grave.

DON HILL'S (511 GREENWICH ST., NEW YORK, NY 10013; HTTP://WWW.DONHILLS.COM)

Owner Don Hill (yes, he's a real dude) was initially inspired by the old-school vibe of Max's Kansas City, and after trying his hand at nightclub life with the East Village's Cat Club, he eventually opened his West Village namesake in 1993. However, it wasn't until the club started attracting the likes of local glam rockers Toilet Boys and the weekly Tiswas dance party in the late '90s that it became a scenester destination. In recent years, the club even hosted the weekly Saturday MisShapes party (until the night closed in fall 2007) after the trio parted ways with original hotspot Luke & Leroy's.

KATE'S JOINT (58 AVENUE B, NEW YORK, NY 10009)

Regardless of whether you're an herbivore or a carnivore, Kate's Joint is *the* place to see and be scene in NYC. To get the most bang for your buck, I recommend the huevos rancheros, which you can snag with a salad and hash browns for only $6.95. Plus, there's a good chance you might run into Moby here for Sunday brunch while he's trying to sop up all the alcohol in his system with an un-turkey dinner and disco fries—and that's totally priceless.

MAX FISH (178 LUDLOW ST., NEW YORK, NY 10002; HTTP:// WWW.MAXFISH.COM)

By now you have probably gathered that there are a lot of bars in downtown Manhattan that are frequented by the local scenesters, but none is more beloved—or infamous—than Max Fish. Located off a once sketchy strip on the Lower East Side, this longstanding watering hole has generated all sorts of outlandish rumors over the years. Did you hear the one about how acoustic troubadour Elliott Smith once got thrown out after hitting someone with a cue ball? Or about the

<178>

time when the fat dude* from *The Sopranos* showed up just before last call and shot pool with the local skaters? Don't forget about when your friend walked in on actor Josh Hartnett while he was getting a blowjob in the bathroom from some drunk chick. Gross, as if the bathrooms weren't enough of a war zone already. . . .

MERCURY LOUNGE (217 E HOUSTON ST., NEW YORK, NY 10002; HTTP://WWW.MERCURYLOUNGENYC.COM)

Much like dozens of other clubs scattered across the country, Mercury Lounge is a hole-in-the-wall venue where most up-and-coming bands from New York City play their first shows. That said, you'll often overhear local scenesters say things like, "I saw the Strokes at Mercury before they even had a record deal," or "I was at Morningwood's first show at Mercury. Were you?" Or, better yet, "Dude, I totally saw Clap Your Hands Say Yeah play Mercury before they even *formed*!" Damn, you got served.

NIAGARA (112 AVENUE A, NEW YORK, NY 10009; HTTP://WWW.NIAGRABAR.COM)

Owned by former Motherfucker promoter Johnny T and ex–D Generation frontman Jesse Malin, Niagara is known for the Joe Strummer mural painted on the wall outside, tattooed DJs spinning rock 'n' roll mood music, and the possibility of seeing Ryan Adams slumped in the corner, slurring his words and drooling. However, if you're worried that Adams might not make an appearance because of his newfound sobriety, wait a week. I'm sure some other former Banana Republic model will break up with him soon enough and drive him to drink—or make really embarrassing breakup videos on YouTube.

OTHER MUSIC (15 E 4TH ST., NEW YORK, NY 10003; HTTP://WWW.OTHERMUSIC.COM)

Other Music can hardly be considered your typical mom-and-pop record store, so when it comes to purchasing music, here's how it works:

---

* Which fat dude from *The Sopranos*? Your guess is as good as mine.

<179>

OTHER MUSIC

Upon walking in, you will immediately be greeted by one of the two employees behind the counter. Most days, said employees will be listening to a noise-rock band from Japan and talking loudly about the review that Ryan Schreiber* gave their new favorite band's latest record on Pitchfork. The chatty clerk will also be in no mood to help you—*especially* if you are looking to buy a record by the sort of act people have actually heard of. In fact, if you ever do something stupid, like, say, ask the staff here if they have the new Coldplay album, please do yourself a favor and immediately stop, drop, and roll. You never know what kind of blunt objects these geeks are going to chuck at you.

Yes, sir, the seemingly mild-mannered employees at Other Music will completely turn on you, scoffing at your pedestrian musical tastes

---

* Ryan Schreiber is the editor in chief of Pitchfork, and a few years ago, he moved from Chicago to Brooklyn. In the process, he became the kind of minor celebrity whom locals whispered about whenever he turned up at shows in the area. Usually, those locals whispering about him were record store clerks. Actually, those people were *only* record store clerks, because, to rest of the world, Schreiber is just some dude with a beard who really likes Man Man.

<180>

before shooting laser beams out of their eyes, which will then turn you into nothing more than a pile of charred ash. Okay, maybe they won't turn you into charred ash, but they'll definitely scoff at you and will then go back to discussing some unknown band on Gold Standard Laboratories that will take the rest of the world months to discover—that is, if they ever discover them at all.

PATRICIA FIELD (302 BOWERY, NEW YORK, NY 10012; HTTP://WWW.PATRICIAFIELD.COM)

For any girl who wishes her life was as glamorous as those of the ladies on *Sex and the City*—which, let's be honest, is, like, *all* girls everywhere—the name "Patricia Field" is synonymous with style and sass. After all, Field was responsible for styling Carrie Bradshaw & Co. with the most fabulous fashions known to man. Carrying everyone from Tripp to Judi Rosen to Field's own signature line, this boutique is wacky carnival of cool. Plus, not only does Andre J., one of the city's most beautiful bearded ladies, work there, but Field herself is known to pop in all the time with her two little white dogs.

SEAGULL (240 W 10TH ST., NEW YORK, NY 10014; HTTP://WWW.SEAGULLHAIR.COM)

Seagull hair salon would be just another overpriced place to get your hair did if not for the fact that Le Tigre guitarist/vocalist Johanna Fateman is a co-owner and sometimes receptionist. No, you won't be able to brag to your friends that a member of Le Tigre totally trimmed your bangs (or, in the case of female bandmate JD Samson, trimmed your mustache), but you *can* brag that someone who is besties with Fateman probably did. Hell, it's better than nothing, right?

A MOMENT OF SILENCE

BROWNIES (169 AVENUE A, NEW YORK, NY 10019; HTTP://WWW.BROWNIESNYC.COM)

Once voted Best Sound per Square Foot and Best Venue to Take Your Little Bro/Sis to for His/Her First Punk Show, Brownies was a fave club for critics and fans alike. To sum up the club in one word, it would be "small." Okay, more like "tiny." I'm talking "crazy fucking miniscule." However, whatever the place lacked in elbow room, it more than made up for in intimacy. Since its opening in 1989, scenesters would come from every borough and jam inside the venue just to catch a glimpse of groups like Superchunk, Crooked Fingers, and Shudder to Think. However, after working in a glorified sardine can for nearly fifteen years and losing shows to burgeoning Brooklyn clubs, the owners decided to revamp the space as a bar sans live music.

Sadly, Brownies officially closed in August 2002, retaining the same ownership and management, who rechristened the space as Hi-Fi the very next month. Sure, the place got a major facelift à la *Extreme Makeover: Home Edition*, but if you step foot inside the East Village haunt today, you can still feel the ghosts of snot-nosed punks past who played there before the 26,000-song MP3 jukebox (the first of its kind) and copper tabletops were installed. Fans mourned but eventually found solace at Hi-Fi, which has made a name for itself by hosting show after-parties and First Taste Tuesdays, where DJs play choice cuts from the week's recent album releases.

April 28, 2003

Bright Eyes frontman Conor Oberst—and the Omaha music scene—breaks through the mainstream media when People *magazine runs a picture of the acoustic troubadour allegedly kissing actress (and serial musicianist) Winona Ryder in a parking lot. The coupling causes major news outlets to focus in on Omaha as the next hipster hot spot, turning an otherwise quiet scene into something of a media circus. The coupling is never officially confirmed and the rumors soon disappear, but it's interesting to note that Ryder eventually goes on to date Oberst's former labelmate Blake Sennett from Rilo Kiley. Sharing is caring, right?*

Omaha, Nebraska

Twenty years ago, you would have never guessed that some of the country's most beloved songwriters would come from the same place that birthed Mannheim Steamroller and TV dinners.* But Omaha eventually developed one of the most revered music scenes, thanks to a whole lot of bleeding heart emo troubadours.

MUSIC PRIMER

Counting Crows frontman Adam Duritz may've been born in Washington, D.C., but he must've been a Midwesterner at heart when he penned the immortal lyrics to what would become one of his band's most beloved songs, "Omaha." Up until the mid-'90s—around the same time that Duritz was dating half the female cast of *Friends* and buying his dreadlocks down at the corner wig shop—O-Town was primarily known for spawning less-than-brag-worthy acts like Larry the Cable Guy and 311, a funk-rock fave of Kappa Sigmas everywhere. However, thanks to a bunch of neighborhood friends who were inspired by the music of Bob Dylan, Tom Waits, and Bruce Springsteen, a *trés* important scene was starting to bubble up somewhere in Middle America.

Many scenesters insist that the "Omaha sound" started to develop

---

* Swanson, an Omaha-based, poultry-centric line of canned and frozen food products, introduced the concept of TV dinners to consumers in 1952. Courses included Salisbury Steak, Classic Fried Chicken, and Mexican-Style Fiesta.

OMAHA, NEBRASKA

when local legends **Slowdown Virginia** formed in 1993. Led by mastermind Tim Kasher—who vacillated between sounding like Eddie Vedder and Barry Gibb—Slowdown Virginia injected a healthy dose of Americana into its brand of alt-indie rock and was the first band in the scene to unite an entire community of budding artists and musicians. Unfortunately, the band only lasted three years, but Kasher wasn't done transforming the musical landscape just yet—and neither was guitarist Ted Stevens, Kasher's classmate at Creighton Preparatory School and future **Cursive** bandmate. Stevens would also try his hand at commanding audiences with his folk-infused group **Lullaby for the Working Class**, in which he played alongside brothers Mike and A.J. Mogis, two Lincoln natives who would later be instrumental in shaping the "Omaha sound."

While playing with Lullaby, Stevens was introduced to another Creighton Prep classmate's geeky younger brother, who happened to be writing heartfelt love songs on his acoustic guitar, despite the fact that the kid: (1) was thirteen and (2) had probably never been in love. Captivated by what he heard, Stevens encouraged the lil' guy to perform at an open-mic night, and in one musical brush stroke, the scene was introduced to the budding genius of Conor Oberst. Not quite ready to strike out on his own, Oberst joined up with buddies Kasher, Robb Nansel, Ben Armstrong (who would later start **Head of Femur**), and two future members of **the Faint** to start **Commander Venus**, a loud, disjointed alt-rock band that garnered enough national attention to get signed by Thick Records. Unfortunately, soon after releasing 1997's *An Uneventful Vacation*, Kasher called it quits to focus more attention on his new project Cursive, and the rest of Commander Venus eventually followed suit.

Rising from the ashes of Slowdown Virginia, Cursive brought Kasher together with former bandmates Matt Maginn (bass) and Stephen Pedersen (guitar) to shape their sound into something that would transcend Slowdown's dingy and unrefined alt-rock roots. Over the years, Kasher would rotate a variety of musicians and instruments in and out, but the core of Cursive's experimental indie-

<187>

rock remained the same throughout releases like *Domestica*, *The Ugly Organ*, and *Happy Hollow*. Art is hard, but change is good. Plus, as if Kasher weren't busy enough, he still found time to focus on his intelligent, folk-tinged, "don't you dare call it a side project" side project **the Good Life** and managed to churn out a new album almost every two years.

While Tim Kasher was writing in Cursive and the Good Life, Conor Oberst started putting out albums under the moniker **Bright Eyes**. Stark yet textured, atonal yet melodic, Oberst was gaining attention in music scenes outside Omaha thanks to constant touring and the release of *Letting Off the Happiness* and *Fevers and Mirrors*.

However, it was his breakthrough release *Lifted or the Story Is in the Soil, Keep Your Ear to the Ground* that found the boy wonder at the center of the mainstream media dial. Songs like "Lover I Don't Have to Love" and "Bowl of Oranges" resonated with audiences and critics alike, making it Saddle Creek's first release to sell more than a hundred thousand copies. (They even celebrated by throwing a party at the local zoo. No joke.) Although Oberst experimented with different sounds (like his short-lived post-punk band **Desaparecidos**), labels (his solo debut was released in August 2008 on Merge

Records), and locales (his temporary residence in NYC's East Village provided much of the inspiration for 2005's *I'm Wide Awake, It's Morning*), he always seems to come back home to Saddle Creek and Omaha.

If there's one word that describes the "Omaha sound," it's "vaired." Whether you're talking about the Faint's dance-punk disco tunes, **Neva Dinova**'s folksy tales of sorrow and despair, or Atlanta transplants **Tilly and the Wall**'s kindergarten-cute indie-pop, all of these bands have equally inspired and contributed to the scene. (Tilly even proved you don't have to have a drummer to be a real-deal indie band. You can use a tap dancer who looks like a slightly less bulbous Beth Ditto. I'm not sure if that's always a good thing, though.) Since the turn of the century, however, bands embodying the "Omaha sound" aren't necessarily from the 68102 zip code: Instead, the scene has newly adopted outsiders like **Nik Freitas**, **Art in Manila**, and San Francisco's **Two Gallants** and treated them like one of its own. With so much musical success to come out of Cornhusker country in the last twenty years, I know it's only a matter of time before tastemakers stop looking for "the next Seattle" and start searching for "the next Omaha."

LABEL CONSCIOUS

When Native Americans occupied the land that would eventually be colonized as Omaha, I'm betting they wouldn't have expected the area to become a hipster haven nearly five hundred years later. But four centuries on, all eyes would turn to the Gate City to the West, thanks in part to a small indie label called **Saddle Creek Records**. Originally named Lumberjack Records, it was started in 1993 by friends Robb Nansel, Justin Oberst, and Ted Stevens as a way to distribute a cassette tape by Justin's dorky-looking younger brother, who just so happened to be a talented singer/songwriter. This rinky-dink, four-track recording, known as *Water*,* would become legendary for two reasons: (1) It served as the first official release of Lumberjack Records, and (2) it marked the acoustic debut by a then-unknown thirteen-year-old musician (who looked like a cross between Harry Potter and Dakota Fanning) named Conor Oberst, who would eventually go by the name of **Bright Eyes**.

In 1996, after Nansel & Co. realized that there was another indie label/distributor going by the Lumberjack moniker, they soon renamed the label Saddle Creek, after the stretch of road that cuts through the east side of midtown Omaha. It was around this time that the Creekers decided to turn the label into a full-fledged business, which was, thankfully, helped along by Nansel and classmate Mike Mogis working the label into a school project for their small business class in college. Instead of just releasing cassette tapes, Saddle Creek evolved into a fully functioning record label that distributed vinyl and CDs. Over the next ten years, nearly every major player in the Omaha scene would release albums on Saddle Creek, including **Slowdown Virginia**, **Commander Venus**, **Cursive**, and **the Faint**. Up until 2002, it looked like the label *only* released albums by Nebraska natives, but that all changed when they released *The Execution of All Things* by **Rilo Kiley**, who hailed from Los Angeles.

Once the seal was broken, Saddle Creek went nationwide: They put out albums by **Azure Ray** (from Athens, Georgia), **Georgie James** (from Washington, D.C.), and **Tokyo Police Club** (from the Great White North of Ontario, Canada); they distributed artists off imprint labels like Conor Oberst's Team Love Records, Range Life Records (which was started by Justin Roelofs, formerly of the Anniversary), and Slumber Party Records; they even opened a music venue and bar in downtown Omaha. Sure, Saddle Creek is straying further and further away from the typical "Omaha sound," but if I didn't know better, I'd think

---

* Unfortunately, *The Water Cassette* has been out of print for years, but thanks to some grainy tape scans and the occasional appearance on eBay, it will forever live on in infamy—much to the chagrin of Conor Oberst, who hits puberty harder on those songs than Peter Brady on "Time to Change."

that the label was giving Warren Buffett a run for his money as the unofficial mayor of the Big O.

WORD PLAY

As many songs by the above bands suggest, there's not much to do on the east end of Nebraska other than pine over lost love. . . . Or drink off a breakup. . . . Or write a song about pining over lost love and drinking off a breakup. Here I breakdown the anatomy of a typical song inspired by this oftentimes lovelorn and drunk scene.

Songwriters from the Big O are all about the Big L, so grandiose gestures of love and affection are preferred—and encouraged. The more over-the-top and unrealistic, the better.
BONUS POINTS: Using phrases like "soul mate," "love of my life," and "the one"
EX: "Well, you walked into the room just like the sun / And woke the caveman from his endless slumber / With the quickness of your arm, you pulled out a paint brush and you painted the sky back to blue" (from "Love Song" off Tilly and the Wall's *Bottoms of Barrels*)

Singer/songwriters from the Omaha scene are totally obsessed with the ninth letter of the alphabet. (That'd be the letter *I*, for any of the slightly illiterate readers out there.) In turn, lyrics should definitely reflect their "enough about me, more about me" mantra.
BONUS POINTS: Taking time out of your precious self-worshipping schedule to grab a pen and paper
EX: "So if you want to be with me / With these things there's no telling / We just have to wait and see / But I'd rather be working for a paycheck / Than waiting to win the lottery / Besides, maybe this time is different / I mean, I really think you like me" (from "First Day of My Life" off Bright Eyes' *I'm Wide Awake, It's Morning*)

You can't call yourself an Omaha-inspired songwriter without writing about how much you love to drink, hate to drink, can't drink enough, or wish you were drunk right now.

BONUS POINTS: Working in the name of an Omaha watering hole like the Dubliner, the Underwood, or Sullivan's

EX: "At Sullivan's, drinking with Justin / He says he's seen my ex-girlfriend / She's back in town and what's worse / He knows where and when she works" (from "Notes in His Pocket" off the Good Life's *Album of the Year*)

In case people aren't already aware of your intimidating intellect, despite the fact that you're constantly dropping your Mensa membership card at social gatherings (accidentally, of course), try name-checking existentialist or postmodernist novelists in your song.

BONUS POINTS: Finding something that rhymes with Dostoevsky

EX: "She led me all over the campus / All the while, I'm asking her questions / She agreed to a cup of coffee / That's when I started to lay it on heavy / Once she learned I studied Dostoevsky, it was in the bag" (from "Into the Fold" off Cursive's *Happy Hollow*)

If there's one thing that musicians from Omaha sing about besides love, liquor, and Charles Bukowski, it's getting laid—or at least the desire to get laid. Feel free to be as vague or specific as possible. This subject matter works especially well if you're in a new wave, dance-punk band.
BONUS POINTS: Having the balls (pun intended) to perform when you write a song called "Erection"
EX: "The feeling of sex is nothing possible yet / A new-wave soldier is standing next to a young nun / The sound of her voice and the handle of the robe / Are getting thinner as the whip begins to speak" (from "Casual Sex" off the Faint's *Blank-Wave Arcade*)

WHERE DO BROKEN HEARTS GO?

I don't know about you, but when I get dumped,* all I want to do is drink boxes of white zinfandel, eat obscene amounts of Hostess Ding Dongs, and take comfort in the crooning of a fellow broken-hearted fool. Whether you're a native of the Big O or are a long-distance admirer, it's easy to find solace in the misery-fueled musing of Omaha artists like Conor Oberst, Tim Kasher, Jake Bellows, and beyond. But once the box of Franzia is tapped, your waistband finally pops, and the tears are wiped away, how well do you really know your Omaha emoters? Can you match the maestros with their lyrical misfortunes? Here's your chance.

Oh, and to keep you on your toes, I've thrown in a wild card in the form of Toni Braxton, my favorite diminutive R&B diva. Why? Because it's my book and I'll "Breathe Again" if I want to.

---

* Not like anyone's ever dumped *me* before . . . I'm just trying to relate to all you poor saps who *have* been deep-sixed. Yeah, I'm empathetic like that. You're welcome.

1. Conor Oberst (Bright Eyes)	**A.** "Mama I tried a thousand times / I'm frozen to the core / Your son is a glorious mess, who wrecks anything he adores / But deep in his center he swears there's a candle just waiting to burn and melt"
2. Tim Kasher (The Good Life)	**B.** "But as the story goes or it is often told, a new day will arise / And all the dance halls will be full of skeletons that are coming back to life / And on a grassy hill the lion will lay down with the lamb / And I won't ever be lonely again / But until that time I think I had better find some disbelief to suspend / Cause I don't want to feel like this again"
3. Joe Knapp (Son Ambulance)	**C.** "Take back that sad word goodbye / Bring back the joy to my life / Don't leave me here with these tears / Come and kiss that pain away / I can't forget the day you left / Time is so unkind / And life is so cruel without you here beside me"
4. Jake Bellows (Neva Dinova)	**D.** "I need a catalyst to rekindle the flame / That once burned where defeat remains"
5. Toni Braxton	**E.** "I was born and I died / Happened right before your eyes and still you wanted something more than silence out of me / I was hiding / I've been lying sick in bed and trying / Now it's too late for perfection / You won't see my face again"
6. Tim Kasher (Cursive)	**F.** "And the night breaks to a thousand different pieces / And they all look like you in the eyes / That's enough, twist the knife and let me die"

ANSWER KEY

1. B, from "I Won't Ever Be Happy Again" off *Don't Be Afraid of Turning the Page* EP, **2.** A, from "What We Fall for When We're Already Down" off *Novena on a Nocturn*, **3.** E, from "An Instant Death" off *Euphemystic*, **4.** F, from "At Least the Pain Is Real" off *Neva Dinova*, **5.** C, from "Un-break My Heart" off *Secrets*, **6.** D, from "The Night I Lose the Will to Fight" off *Domestica*

"I'VE FALLEN . . . AND I CAN'T GET UP!"

As I mentioned before, there's nothing like a glass of wine—boxed or bottled—to ease a broken heart. In fact, it seems like the more inconsolable you are, the more wine you'll probably need to numb the pain. Seeing as many Omahans have made a career out of heartbreak, I'm guessing that many of them are members of numerous wine-of-the-month clubs—at least that would easily explain why every time bands like the Faint and Omaha adoptee Rilo Kiley perform, they can't seem to stay on their feet.

For example, every time Conor Oberst zones out and starts to "feel the music," Conor fall down, go boom. Sometimes he flips backwards over an amp, other times he does a Tasmanian Devil–esque maneuver because there are cables wrapped around his feet; either way, if you're going to be a musician in this town, you're going to need some pointers on how to remain erect. (Get your mind outta the gutters, people. You know what I mean. Geez . . .) And so, whether you pre-partied a little too hard or you zone out during a killer glockenspiel solo, here are some tips to get you through a gig—concussion-free.

1. IF YOU'RE ABOUT TO FALL INTO A HAZARDOUS AREA, TRY TO PROPEL YOUR BODY AWAY FROM SAID HAZARD.

Most Omaha bands have about forty-two people on stage at any one time (give or take a glockenspiel player, or something as equally ridiculous as that), and with that many musicians comes a shit-ton of large, heavy equipment. With each inch of the stage littered with amps, cords, stands, instruments, pedals, beer bottles, wine glasses, and possibly whiskey carousels (depending on whether one of Tim Kasher's bands is playing), one small misstep and you're in for world of trouble—and, more important, pain. Therefore, if you feel yourself on the verge of taking a nosedive because you've accidentally slipped on the butt of an American Spirit or that last shot of Maker's Mark is starting to give you a gnarly case of the spins, try to aim your face-plant *away* from anything with sharp edges. Not only will you avoid looking like a clumsy idiot, but you'll also prevent suffering from any gruesome face lacerations. After all, why waste a perfectly good-looking comb-over on a cerebral contusion?

2. LOWER YOUR CENTER OF GRAVITY.

The bigger you are, the harder you fall, so if you're like Blake Sennett from Rilo Kiley, then there's a good chance you barely meet the height requirement to ride the Big Ohhhh! at Nebraska's Fun-Plex Amusement Park. That said, all you basically have to do if you're in danger of taking a tumble is simply bend your knees and you're pretty much already on the floor. However, if you find yourself eye-to-eye with someone like Criteria's Stephen Pedersen (whom I consider to be the Yao Ming of Saddle Creek), then prepare yourself for about thirty seconds of freefall before you hit the ground—that is, unless you lower your center of gravity. If you feel yourself starting to topple, widen your stance to gain stability. That should save you from taking out a Mogis brother or two.

3. AVOID LANDING ON YOUR HANDS.

Creekers have long been accused of having limp wrists, so this shouldn't be *that* hard to remember.

4. WHILE FALLING, TWIST OR ROLL YOUR BODY TO THE SIDE

Say you're Tim Kasher and you're coming to the front of the stage to get the crowd riled up for the bridge in "The Casualty." One faulty misstep and you could be hanging ten into a steel barricade. (Talk about potential *casualties*! Ba-dum-bum.) As to avoid getting your 'nads in a bunch—and possibly being unable to procreate later in life—try to twist or roll your body to the side so you reduce the impact on your neck, skull, and spine. The last thing you want to do is end your set with a full-frontal belly flop like the ginger-haired fat kid in *The Sandlot*. Damn, I get a water burn just thinking about it.

MAPPING OUT OMAHA

ARC STUDIOS (5912 MAPLE ST., OMAHA, NE 68104)

Production maestro Mike Mogis calls this newly renovated recording studio home after moving the legendary production HQ (Presto! Recording Studios) that he ran with his brother A.J. from Lincoln to Omaha in 2007. Now co-owned by Bright Eyes brethren Conor Oberst, ARC is located in an old indoor basketball court and boasts two large control rooms, a MIDI room, a lounge, a game room, a guest room, an indoor swimming pool, a paintball course, and a full-service salon and spa. (Just kidding about the paintball and spa part.) In the meantime, the studio has been christened by artists like Cursive (who recorded the follow-up to 2006's *Happy Hollow* here) and Omaha newcomers Thunder Power.

BROTHERS LOUNGE (3812 FARNAM ST., OMAHA, NE 68131)

Located a stone's throw from the Saddle Creek offices, it's no wonder that Brothers Lounge is the scene's watering hole of choice. Run by two local punks, Brothers remains one of the few places in town that serves absinthe *and* has a killer jukebox selection. (Anyone up for a cut off Big Black's *Songs About Fucking*?) Plus, this retro dive is forever immortalized as one of the reasons Tim Kasher misses this city[*] in the Good Life rarity "Haunted Homecoming."

CREIGHTON PREPARATORY SCHOOL (7400 WESTERN AVE., OMAHA, NE 68114; HTTP://WWW.CREIGHTONPREP.CREIGHTON.EDU)

Besides being soldiers for Christ and performing missionary work, those Jesuits sure like to rock out to Americana music, huh? If that weren't true, what other reason would there be for so many Omaha scenesters to pass through the hallowed halls of this fine Jesuit educational establishment? Notable alumni include Tim Kasher, Cursive's Matt Maginn, Conor Oberst, and Criteria's Steve Pedersen, just to name a few. If you're sick of me name-dropping artists on Saddle Creek, then you'll probably be interested to know that the flying kid who used to date the cheerleader on *Heroes* also went here and, perhaps more important, so did director Alexander Payne of *Sideways*, *About Schmidt*, and *Election* fame.

---

[*] In 2007, Kasher traded in his Central Standard Time roots for the PST network of sunny Los Angeles. I'm guessing you can probably find him eating at the Ivy, shopping on Robertson Boulevard, or drinking in the VIP section at Les Deux. No wonder it was here that he was inspired to write a screenplay, which ultimately inspired the Good Life album *Help Wanted Nights*. I heard the album was supposed to be titled *Help Wanted Perez Hilton*, but that was too wordy.

DRASTIC PLASTIC (1209 HOWARD ST., OMAHA, NE 68102)

Though slightly more expensive than the Antiquarium (see "A Moment of Silence" below), Drastic Plastic offers a pretty extensive collection of vinyl, new and used CDs, band T-shirts, and movies. Even more impressive is their inventory of pro-Nebraska goodies. Plus, if that weren't enough, owner Mike Howard recently launched Drastic Plastic Records, which released special-edition vinyl by the Toasters and the Briggs. (Caveat emptor: Apparently, there's another Drastic Plastic Records whose biggest artist is a band called Rock 'n' Roll Monkey and the Robots. If you've accidentally stumbled upon their Web page, abort mission. You are totally in the wrong place.)

MCFOSTER'S NATURAL KIND CAFÉ (302 S 38TH ST., OMAHA, NE 68131; HTTP://WWW.MCFOSTERS.COM)

In a city known for Omaha Steaks, it's hard to find some solid veggie-friendly cuisine. (Here is where I'd insert a really funny and inappropriate joke about how savory Omaha Steaks are, but I'd prefer not to have PETA picket my future book signings, so just use your imagination.) Thankfully, there's McFoster's Natural Kind Café, which serves traditional vegetarian fare in addition to free-range chicken dishes and fresh seafood. The menu's a little hippy-dippy ("happy hummus" would go great with a "kind salad," don't cha think?), but it's easy to look past the Café's cheesiness when they partake in many great environmentally conscious activities like recycling all waste glass, tin, paper, aluminum, and plastic, using products that are organic or locally grown whenever possible, and offering a 10 percent discount when you bring in your own container for takeout. Kick over the Hackey Sack, brah.

SOKOL UNDERGROUND (2234 S 13TH ST., OMAHA, NE 68108; HTTP://WWW.SOKOLUNDERGROUND.COM)

Headlining Sokol Underground is a rite of passage for any up-and-coming band—regardless of whether or not the group is from Omaha. Rich in history, the building was erected in the 1920s in order to offer vari-

OMAHA, NEBRASKA

ous social activities to the area's burgeoning Czech population. Today, the auditorium that houses the Underground also plays host to party rentals and various gymnastics classes. (No, *seriously.*) Playing the Underground is *such* a big deal, in fact, that the venue has inspired name-drops in songs like the Faint's "Amorous in Bauhaus Fashion" and They Might Be Giants' "Sokol Auditorium." Take that, House of Blues.

THE FOUNDRY (6051 MAPLE ST., OMAHA, NE 68104; HTTP://WWW.OMAHAFOUNDRY.COM)

If you're looking to slurp down a frozen whipped decaf mochaccino soy latte, then don't bother going to the Foundry. But if you're interested in serving your community and scoring a free cup of java as a bonus, then you're in the right place. This self-proclaimed "pseudo coffeehouse" donates any profit back into the Omaha community through local charity organizations and is run entirely by volunteers. It kind of makes Ty Pennington and his posse of *Extreme Makeover: Home Edition* look like a bunch of self-centered assholes, huh?

THE SLOWDOWN (729 N 14TH ST., OMAHA, NE 68102; HTTP://WWW.THESLOWDOWN.COM)

Named after local scene legends Slowdown Virginia and started by Saddle Creek business guys Robb Nansel and Jason Kulbel, the Slowdown has quickly become Omaha's newest must-play music venue—and Sokol Underground's biggest competitor. Bright Eyes was the first band to perform at the venue, on June 7, 2007, and in the time since, an eclectic mix of groups like the Rentals, Tilly and the Wall, As I Lay Dying, and Rilo Kiley have all graced the stage. Not bad for the brain child of two dudes who used to work at Blockbuster Video.

THE WAITING ROOM LOUNGE (6212 MAPLE ST., OMAHA, NE 68104; HTTP://WWW.WAITINGROOMLOUNGE.COM)

Unlike most places in the Omaha scene, the Waiting Room Lounge is *not* owned by or affiliated with Saddle Creek Records. Instead, this hole-in-the-wall bar and venue is owned and operated by 1% Productions, a two-man concert promotion team that books shows all over Omaha, Lincoln, and neighboring Council Bluffs, Iowa. Although the club is starkly decorated and only holds 250 people max, the Waiting Room is earning major cred points for not only booking great shows but also supporting local talent.

A MOMENT OF SILENCE

ANTIQUARIUM BOOKSTORE (1215 HARNEY ST., OMAHA, NE 68102)

When the Antiquarium opened its doors in the early '70s, Omaha had never seen anything like it. Not only did the store sell rare, used, and hard-to-find titles, but it also played host to Youth for Peace meetings, poetry readings, musical performances, and other acts of activism. Located downtown in the Old Market district, this literary Mecca occupied four floors in a nondescript building on Harney Street: The top floor was an art gallery/reading room; the second and first floors held the nearly one-hundred-thousand-piece book inventory, in addition to stacks of magazines and comic books; and, finally, the basement was occupied by the Antiquarium Record Shop, which was filled with an overwhelming selection of vinyl, tapes, and CDs, plus a special "local" section for bands from the hood (which basically included, like, every release on Saddle Creek).

Sure, the place looked like your grandparents' crawlspace and smelled like a combination of mothballs and feet (supposedly because the owner never wore socks), but this Omaha landmark was close to the heart of scenesters like Conor Oberst (who can even be seen—John Lennon glasses and all—in the DVD extras of the *Spend an Evening with Saddle Creek* documentary gushing about how the Antiquarium is "the best music store in the country"). No wonder the record shop used to keep a handmade copy of Bright Eyes' *Letting*

Off the Happiness on vinyl* in a glass display case. Unfortunately, in September 2007, the owners of the city's beloved bookstore decided to move the operation south after buying an old school building in Brownsville, Nebraska. Although the new location is only about seventy miles away from Omaha, it's safe to say that the scene will still be mourning the loss for a long time to come.

---

* Audiophile footnote: This über-rare edition of Bright Eyes' sophomore album—which featured yellow, green, red, and pink bubbles on the cover—was limited to three hundred copies and was handmade and numbered by Conor and the dudes at Saddle Creek. The last time I checked, this LP sold for more than two hundred dollars on eBay. True story.

August 21, 2004

For many scene purists, the music dies when the owners of the Fireside Bowl decide to pull the plug on all future concerts at the venue and, instead, devote their attention to turning the space into a full-time, high-end bowling alley. As a direct result, emo fans everywhere cry a little more than usual today.

Chicago, Illinois

If you're talking about scenes that helped shape the musical under-ground as we know it today, you can't leave out Chicago, the backdrop for Midwestern emo and a whole lot of John Cusack movies.

MUSIC PRIMER

Chicago is a funny town—and not just because it's home to the Second City improvisational theater, which has launched the careers of comedians like Steve Carell and Tina Fey. No, it's funny because the scenesters here really think they're the shit. Sure, they might be pastier than their long-lost Los Angeles neighbors and they might move slower than their Energizer Bunny brethren in New York City, but Chicagoans aren't intimidated. The glitz and glamour of the Big Apple and City of Angels mean nothing to these Oprah-loving snobs, especially when it comes to being loud and proud about their Midwestern music pride.

If we take a trip in the way-back machine, the early '90s started out by ushering in the mega-popular industrial movement, which included bands like **Ministry**, **My Life with the Thrill Kill Kult**, and **Pailhead**. Fans of this type of heavy, experimental music usually wore all black, accessorized with dog collars, and studied forensic pathology in their spare time—you know, just for fun. In direct contrast to that, on the other side of the underworld, the Chicago music scene became taken with a group named **Smashing Pump-**

kins, which was basically a brood of record-store clerks making a weird blend of psychedelic post-punk. Their lead singer looked like an early Kim Fowley, but with hair like Jackie Collins; their bassist was reminiscent of a human Blythe doll; the guitarist resembled that of any Asian stereotype that could probably get me sued; and their drummer looked like someone's middle-aged uncle who just happened to stroll into a practice. Over the next ten years, the quartet put out six albums with the original lineup (or close to it) and in 2007 managed a quasi-reunion tour and album (*Zeitgeist*) , which really consisted of only Billy Corgan and his uncle, *er*, Jimmy Chamberlain. Some reunion.

While Corgan & Co. sang about Siamese dreams and cherubs, fellow scenesters **Veruca Salt** were proving that you didn't need a male member to pick up a guitar—unless that member was gonna be in your backing band. Playing just as hard as all the boys, Veruca Salt hit mainstream success almost immediately after signing to Geffen Records and releasing hit singles like "Seether" (off its debut album *American Thighs*) and "Volcano Girls" (from the follow-up *Eight Arms to Hold You*), the latter of which was featured as the opening to the 1999 film *Jawbreaker*. Speaking of soundtracks, thanks to Quentin Tarantino's 1994 cult-classic crime drama *Pulp Fiction*, Chicago trio **Urge Overkill** managed to snag some chart time with their remake of Neil Diamond's "Girl, You'll Be A Woman Soon," which made it all the way to the Billboard Top 50 and finally made it cool for people to like Neil Diamond again. (Even though the release of *Saving Silverman*—a film based around a poor schmuck in a Diamond tribute band—would threaten to destroy that very thought a mere seven years later.)

Toward the end of the '90s, alternative rock was beginning to wane. Pop acts like *N SYNC and Christina Aguilera were bum-rushing radio and video airwaves and the musical soundscape was starting to become more desperate than Tara Reid outside Mr. Chow. Not to worry, though, because a quiet—and emotional—rebellion was beginning to take place in the Chicago suburbs. Mid-level emo up-

starts like **Braid** and **Cap'n Jazz**, in addition to punk peers **Alkaline Trio** and **the Lawrence Arms**, would inspire future scene figureheads like Tim McIlrath and Pete Wentz. The two gents had been sharing the stage in tons of shitty punk and hardcore bands (like **Racetraitor, .baxter.,** and **Arma Angelus**), but it was only when they decided to part way and form bands that were actually good—and accessible to more than the meathead dudes from FSU who worked the door at the Knights of Columbus Hall in Arlington Heights—that things really heated up in the scene.

For Rise Against, a Clash-style punk band with a political consciousness, McIlrath was recruited by bassist Joe Principe from fellow hardcore hometown heroes 88 Fingers Louie, who had already lined up fellow Louie bandmate and guitarist Dan "Mr. Precision" Wleklinski in addition to drummer Brandon Barnes. The band released two albums on Fat Wreck Chords (and traded out nearly a dozen guitar players) before making the major-label move to Geffen Records and putting out the most successful album of its career,

2006's *The Sufferer & the Witness*, which featured everyone's favorite anti-logging jam "Ready to Fall."* At the same time the members of Rise Against were becoming inadvertent rock stars—and activists—McIlrath's former Arma Angelus bandmate Pete Wentz had cracked the mainstream emo code with his band **Fall Out Boy**. Known for the mellifluous voice of one Patrick Stump and obnoxiously long song titles courtesy of Wentz, FOB hit the mainstream jackpot with the release of 2005's *From Under the Cork Tree*; however, some argue that the band didn't *really* make it big until pictures of Wentz's naughty bits landed all over the Internet in 2006, making Wentz and Fall Out Boy a household name.

The infamous bassist and his bandmates sure seemed to enjoy the perks that came along with success (expensive gear, super-famous baby mamas, illegally ionic flat-irons, etc. . . .), but the band definitely shared the wealth with friends like **the Plain White Ts**, who scored one-hit-wonder status with "Hey There Delilah," a song that united Hot Topic shoppers and soccer moms alike. Let's also not forget **the Academy Is . . .** , who *wished* they scored one-hit-wonder status with *any* song off 2007's ill-fated *Santi*. Oh, and there's also **the Hush Sound**, which toured with Fall Out Boy numerous times and was one of the first bands signed to Wentz's imprint label Decaydance.

Who will be leading the next stampede in the Chicago music scene? That has yet to be seen. All we know is that their parents better have some bank because twelve-passenger vans aren't going to buy themselves, are they?

---

* The video clip for "Ready to Fall" was directed by Kevin Kerslake (Nirvana, Faith No More) and featured the members of Rise Against performing amidst scenes of tortured animals and environmental hazards. The video is hard to watch for two reasons: (1) The footage of dolphins caught in fishermen nets is absolutely heartbreaking, and (2) if you look closely, you can see that lead singer Tim McIlrath has two different colored eyes—one blue, one brown. Totally freaky.

LABEL CONSCIOUS

The Chicago scene as you know it today wouldn't exist if not for the hard work, determination, and drive of a couple forward-thinking music fanatics who decided to start two of the landscape's most influential indie record labels— **Touch and Go Records** and **Victory Records**. T&G originally started in 1981 as a magazine put out by Tesco Vee, former frontman of **the Meatmen**, but soon evolved into a label after

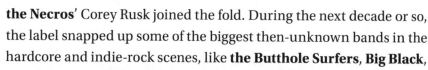

the Necros' Corey Rusk joined the fold. During the next decade or so, the label snapped up some of the biggest then-unknown bands in the hardcore and indie-rock scenes, like **the Butthole Surfers**, **Big Black**, and **the Jesus Lizard**. T&G took a page from the Factory Records rulebook and set up 50-50 deals (splitting all profits down the middle once the artist recoups promotion and production costs) and oral contracts with artists, both of which were far from the norm.

The label currently boasts one of the indie scene's most diverse rosters to date. **Naked Raygun** and **Slint** have experienced newfound popularity after launching successful reunions; **Blonde Redhead** and **the Black Heart Procession** continue to release albums and tour—they've collectively put out a total of fifteen albums, not counting EPs and singles; **the Yeah Yeah Yeahs** and **TV on the Radio** might not be on the label anymore, but they both grew into themselves by releasing seminal recordings for the label; finally, newer signings like **CocoRosie** and **Crystal Antlers** are the perfect argument for those naysayers who complain about the state of music today. Suck it, haters.

Speaking of haters, we can't think of anyone in the industry who attracts as many as Victory Records and founder/head honcho Tony Brummel. In 1989, with little cash and less experience in the biz, Brummel took to waiting tables until his empire grew. Four years later, after the unexpected success of hardcore bands like **Earth Crisis**, **Snapcase,** and **Integrity**, Brummel was finally able to devote all of his attention to Victory and find more underground bands that wouldn't remain so for long. Those bands would include **Atreyu**, **Taking Back Sunday**, **Hawthorne Heights**, **Aiden**, and **Silverstein**, all of which contributed to the rough-and-tumble "Victory sound" often talked about by fans and industry insiders.

However, as Victory grew more and more successful, Brummel's business tactics were soon called into question and some of his biggest sellers wanted out. Lawyers were called, lawsuits were filed, and some bands ceased to release music for years at a time. This is where things get kinda tricky, because I definitely *don't* want the big bulldog (aka Tony) to open a can of whoop-ass on my book-writing tush, so if you want to Google "Victory Records + litigation," be my guest!

MO' MONEY, MO' PROBLEMS

For labels like Touch and Go and Victory to be so successful, they must sell a mountain of records, many of which are snatched up by suburban Chicago's teenage mafia. It's not easy being raised upper-middle-class by parents in the 28-percent tax bracket. No way, Jose. (Oh, sorry. We were just telling Jose, the pool boy, to scrub down the hot tub.) With so many members of Chicago bands coming from the 'burbs, let's take a look at what exactly they're rebelling against, so they can write perfectly crafted songs about girls who won't answer their text messages.

OBESITY

Rich kids don't take public transportation. That's *soooo* known. Instead, they arrive by chauffeured car, limo, plane, yacht, Segway, and

Siberian huskies, like Cuba Gooding, Jr., in *Snow Dogs*. Think about it: If you don't have to travel one mile uphill both ways in the snow to get to where you're going, how are you going to burn any calories? (Look no further than oil heir Jason "Gummi Bear" Davis for proof.)

SUPERFICIALITY

Do your peeps like you for you, or because you've got more dough than Charm City Cakes? We might never know the answer, but I'd like to defer to Joel Madden—Good Charlotte frontman, Nicole Richie's baby daddy, and former Mensa member—for the real answer: "Girls don't like guys. Girls like cars and money." Truer words were never spoken, brosef.

CURFEWS

They suck—no matter how many Benjamins you have in your wallet.

DRESS CODE

When you've got money, people expect you to look the part. It's that conformist attitude that makes hardcore-obsessed kids from the suburbs migrate to the city and pick up matching pairs of black Tripp jeans, black Converse high tops, and Big Black T-shirts.

CHICAGO, ILLINOIS

RULES

Rules are so stupid—and when you break 'em, it's like parents go bal-listic and stuff. What gives? Okay, so maybe you snuck out of your house, stole your parents' Bentley (and driver), and hoofed it to a local basement show where your friend's band was playing, and the car just *happened* to have a run in with an opossum and a handle of Sunny D. How is that *your* fault? Gawd. Now you're totally grounded and can't leave your room all weekend. What's a kid to do when your room *only* has a forty-six-inch plasma screen TV, DVD player, PowerBook computer, VHS player, Wii, laserdisc player, Sony PlayStation 3, minidisk player, refrigerator, hiba-chi, snow-cone machine, hot tub, movie-style popcorn maker, Sidekick 12 (which doesn't even exist yet), and more. So. Not. Fair.

ALL IN THE FAMILY

No matter where your hood is in and around the Windy City, Chica-go's music scene is an incestuous one. Here we'll map out the city's family tree and how bands like Arma Angelus and Slapstick eventually lead to the formation of heavy hitters like Rise Against, Fall Out Boy, and Alkaline Trio.

.BAXTER. (Tim McIlrath, Neil Hen-nessy, Geoff Reu)
88 FINGERS LOUIE (Joe Principe, Mr. Precision, Glen Porter)
ALKALINE TRIO (Matt Skiba, Dan Andriano, Glen Porter, Rob Doran)
ARMA ANGELUS (Pete Wentz, Tim McIlrath, Jay Jancetic)
BREAK THE SILENCE (Mr. Precision)
COLOSSAL (Neil Hennessy, Rob Kellenberger, Eli Caterer)
DUVALL (Rob Kellenberger, Eli Caterer, Josh Caterer)

EXTINCTION (Neeraj Kane, Jay Jancetic, Pete Wentz)
FALL OUT BOY (Pete Wentz)
HOLY ROMAN EMPIRE (Geoff Reu, Jay Jancetic, Neeraj Kane)
NAKED RAYGUN (Pierre Kezdy)
RISE AGAINST (Tim McIlrath, Joe Principe, Todd Mohney)
SLAPSTICK (Dan Andriano, Brendan Kelly, Matt Stamps, Rob Kellenberger, Rob DePaola, Dan Hanaway)
SMOKING POPES (Eli Caterer, Josh Caterer)
STRIKE UNDER (Pierre Kezdy)
SUNDOWNER (Chris McCaughan)
THE BROADWAYS (Rob Kellenberger, Rob DePaola, Chris McCaughan, Dan Hanaway)
THE FALCON (Todd Mohney, Dan Andriano, Rob Kellenberger)
THE HONOR SYSTEM (Rob DePaola, Tyler Wiseman, Chris Carr, Dan Hanaway, Tim McIlrath)
THE KILLING TREE (Tim McIlrath, Todd Mohney, Geoff Reu)
THE LAWRENCE ARMS (Neil Hennessy, Brendan Kelly)
TUESDAY (Matt Stamps, Dan Andriano)
WHALE/HORSE (Chris Carr, Dan Hanaway)

MAPPING OUT CHICAGO

ARAGON BALLROOM (1106 W LAWRENCE AVE., CHICAGO, IL 60640; HTTP://WWW.ARAGON.COM)

Located in Uptown Chicago, the Aragon Ballroom first opened in 1926 and soon became the most famous dance hall in America. As decades passed, things evolved; those who swarmed the floor to jitterbug to Glenn Miller soon gave way to those forming circle pits at AFI. It's no wonder that, in recent years, the venue has been rechristened as the Aragon *Brawl*room by frequent showgoers.

CLANDESTINE INDUSTRIES (952 W NEWPORT AVE., CHICAGO, IL 60657; HTTP://WWW.CLANDESTINEINDUSTRIES.COM)

Fall Out Boy bassist and mega-mogul Pete Wentz has always been something of a fashion maven, so it's no wonder he decided to take his reputation as a trendsetter to the next level by opening this Lakeview boutique. Not only does the store sell clothing from Wentz's Clandestine line, but it also houses a full-service salon (which is led by stylist Ben Mollin, runner-up on the first season of Bravo's *Shear Genius*) and the Batheart Bar, a station that allows buyers to turn their gear into one-of-a-kind pieces of wearable art.

DUNKIN' DONUTS (3200 N CLARK ST., CHICAGO, IL 60657; HTTP://WWW.DUNKINDONUTS.COM)

Lovingly referred to as "Punkin' Donuts," this locale has been a punk hangout since suspicious-looking, leather-clad skinheads started frequenting there in the early '80s. Come for the French crullers, stay for the opportunity to get frisked by cops in the parking lot.

GOLD STAR BAR (1755 W DIVISION ST., CHICAGO, IL 60622)

Located in the heart of Ukrainian Village, Gold Star is a pit stop for hipsters and local college douchebags alike who enjoy sitting at patio furniture *indoors*, eating free popcorn, and screaming over Ministry blaring on the jukebox. Luckily, the drinks aren't over-priced, and you can still run into local punk celebs there—like the dudes in Rise Against, who filmed part of the video for "Swing Life Away" here.

L&L TAVERN (3207 N CLARK ST., CHICAGO, IL 60657)
Back in the late '90s, on any given night—or day—you could find the dudes from the Lawrence Arms tending bar while members of Alkaline Trio huddled around the jukebox, possibly arguing about which Naked Raygun or Johnny Cash song to play. Now it's simply a favorite for traveling musicians looking for a post-show good time. Plus, to prove its punk legendry, the bar has even spawned an offshoot rock band called the L&L All Stars.

METRO (3730 N CLARK ST., CHICAGO, IL 60613; HTTP:// WWW.METROCHICAGO.COM)
You're officially worthless in the Chicago scene if you haven't seen—or played—a show at Metro. The club grew in notoriety after bands like Smashing Pumpkins and Veruca Salt stretched their stage legs here in the early '90s and has continued the buzz-worthy tradition with bands like OK Go making their mark at Metro way before mainstream audiences caught on. And who could forget the famous local joke: "What has twelve hundred legs and no pubic hair? The crowd at a Kill Hannah concert at Metro."

RAINBO CLUB (1150 N DAMEN AVE., CHICAGO, IL 60622)
If you can get past the club's hipster and modelizer clientele, then you can appreciate Rainbo's redeeming qualities like the functioning photo booth and cash-only bar. Note to self: When Joan of Arc's Tim Kinsella *isn't* on tour, he can often be found bartending here, so feel free to come and throw batteries at him—or beg him to sign your Cap'n Jazz *Nothing Dies with Blue Skies* 7-inch split.

RECKLESS RECORDS (3161 N BROADWAY ST., CHICAGO, IL 60657; HTTP://WWW.RECKLESS.COM)

While the Broadway Street location is Reckless's landmark store, the Wicker Park one is nearly right next to where the fictional Championship Vinyl was filmed in *High Fidelity*. If the gawk factor alone doesn't get you in the door, then how about an awe-inspiring indie section that would leave even the most snobbish and elitist Pitchfork reader speechless?

THE GINGERMAN TAVERN (3740 N CLARK ST., CHICAGO, IL 60613)

Parking's a bitch but well worth the aggravation once you step inside this low-key, low-lit bar, which is located a stone's throw away from the Metro. Amidst a bevy of cheesy and frat-fueled sports bars, the Gingerman has been described as the "least date-rapey bar in Wrigleyville." That's always a plus in my book.

VIC THEATRE (3145 N SHEFFIELD AVE., CHICAGO, IL 60657; HTTP://WWW.VICTHEATRE.COM)

Caveat emptor: The bathrooms here are beyond disgusting, so don't leave the house without an iron stomach—or a colostomy bag. That said, if seeing bands like Cat Power and the Dresden Dolls isn't your scene ('cause, you know, you have *negative* taste in music), try hoofing it next door to the Vic's bratty little brother the Brew & View, which has three bars and shows your favorite cult classic films.

VINTAGE VINYL RECORDS (925 DAVIS ST., EVANSTON, IL, 60201; HTTP://WWW.VVMO.COM)

Vintage Vinyl isn't just a dingy record store—it's a pop culture landmark. In addition to providing inspiration for the fictitious Championship Vinyl in *High Fidelity*, Vintage Vinyl is also featured in novel *The Time Traveler's Wife* by Audrey Niffenegger. If you like to read things other than the replies on your Twitter account, then this might be slightly impressive.

A MOMENT OF SILENCE

THE FIRESIDE BOWL (2648 W FULLERTON AVE., CHICAGO, IL 60647; HTTP://WWW.FIRESIDEBOWL.COM)

For those unfamiliar with the Fireside, start with any of the *Live at the Fireside Bowl* albums by bands like Swingin' Utters, Anti-Flag, the Casualties, Slapstick, or Against All Authority. Come to think of it, it's pretty safe to say that nearly *every* band in your iTunes has probably played—and rocked—the good ol' Fireside. Ironically enough, that's what led to the venue's demise. Back in the day, the Fireside was known for its all-ages shows, five-dollar ticket prices, and diverse

CHICAGO, ILLINOIS

lineups, which eventually wreaked too much havoc on the lanes and caused the ultimate shutdown.

Put the Kleenex down, kiddies. All is not lost. The bowling portion of the Fireside got a major makeover and is actually good-looking, so much so that the lanes attracted the likes of Jennifer Aniston and Vince Vaughn when they shot scenes from *The Break-Up* here. If that doesn't offer you much solace, how about this: Brian Peterson, who booked and set up shows during Fireside's heyday, has taken his mind-blowing booking abilities to other rooms in and around the city (like Subterranean, Reggies Rock Club, and the Knights of Columbus in Arlington Heights, where Fall Out Boy played many of its first shows together). Sure, you may've missed seeing Q and Not U play with Denali and Chin Up Chin Up, but you've still got a chance to see the next underground post-punk band at Fireside-approved venues like Logan Square Auditorium, the Bottom Lounge, and South Union Arts—and that sense of hope is way more than we can say about the current state of Vince Vaughn's career.

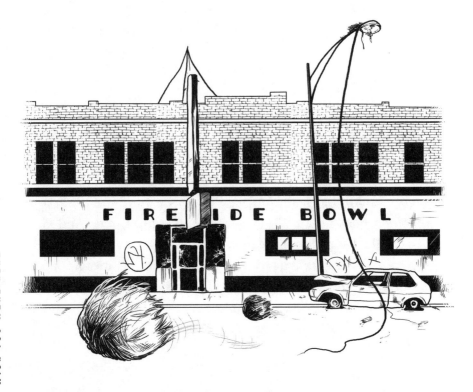

November 2, 2004

After a bitter battle for control between co-owners, Minneapolis rock club First Avenue files for Chapter 7 bankruptcy, lays off over a hundred employees, and officially closes its doors, much to the chagrin and dismay of local concertgoers. Troubles started a year earlier, when rumors of financial difficulties surfaced and came to a head in June 2004 when San Francisco–based co-owner Allan Fingerhut fired talent booker Steve McClellan and business manager Jack Meyers, the two men widely considered to be responsible for the club's success.

Over the next couple weeks, McClellan and Meyers (along with overwhelming support from the surrounding music scene) attempt to evict Fingerhut and reclaim Minneapolis's most beloved venue. Finally, on November 12, a U.S. bankruptcy court rules in favor of McClellan and Meyers, and First Avenue reopens the very next weekend. Victory was theirs and to celebrate, they book—wait for it—GWAR and Los Lonely Boys. Guess you win some and you lose some.

The Twin Cities

The scene in the Twin Cities has provided a safe haven for a whole slew of heavy drinkers and aspiring rock critics for nearly two decades now. In this chapter, let's examine what continues to inspire local bands to churn out some of the best alt-rock to date—and why they can't seem to do so without hitting the bottle so hard.

MUSIC PRIMER

When you visit Minnesota, some residents may tell you that the state's name translates to "10,000 lakes" in Sioux; others seem to think that it means "cloudy water," which makes sense once you look at the condition of the Minnesota River. Either way, I'm smitten by the state's cute, nasal accents, shitty weather, and wacky roadside attractions.* Most importantly, though, I've gotta give it up for the Twin Cities— Minneapolis and St. Paul, for those who failed geography—and their ever-evolving music scenes.

Up until the late '70s, the rest of the country didn't give two flying farts about bands from the Twin Cities. That all changed, though, with the formation of two groups that would go on to define an alt-rock generation: **Hüsker Dü** and **the Replacements**. The Dü's sound was hard to describe—mostly because it was an amalgamation of crunchy, hardcore-inspired, and melodic post-punk—but its DIY methodol-

---

* I suggest the Spam Museum (in Austin, Minnesota) or the World's Largest Ball of Twine (in Darwin, Minnesota).

<222>

ogy was hard to miss. The trio—vocalist/guitarist Bob Mould, bass-ist Greg Norton, and drummer Grant Hart—toured tirelessly behind now-classic albums like *Zen Arcade*, *New Day Rising*, and *Flip Your Wig* until they conquered Minneapolis and the rest of the country, which promptly grew child-molester-like mustaches, much like the one rocked by drummer Grant Hart. In fact, Hüsker Dü was one of the first underground bands approached by a major label (Warner Bros.), and one of the few that managed to maintain its identity without sell-ing out to the Man.

At the same time Mould & Co. were burning up the *CMJ* charts, the Replacements were also being courted by the majors (Sire, a sub-sidiary of Warner Bros.) after earning a loyal local following based on their raw, heartfelt alt-rock songs and raucous live shows. The band—

guitarist/vocalist Paul Westerberg, guitarist Bob Stinson, bassist Tommy Stinson—were known as much for being shit-faced as they were for carefully crafting songs that defied simple hooks and genres. During the height of the band's success, it released two critically acclaimed albums, *Tim* and *Pleased to Meet Me*, which included seminal recordings like "Bastards of Young,"* "Left of the Dial," and "Alex Chilton."

For a hot second, thanks to the Mats and the Dü, all eyes seemed to be on the bands emerging from the Twin Cities. Groups like **Babes in Toyland**, **Soul Asylum,** and **the Jayhawks**, and later **Semisonic** and **Marcy Playground**, revved up like a runaway train (pun intended), though they never reached the same level of local stardom or influence as Hüsker Dü and the Replacements, who both imploded by 1987 and 1991, respectively. Mould went on to form the Dü-esque alt-rock band Sugar before embarking on a solo career; Westerberg went out on his own as well, scoring another blip of success by contributing two lovelorn tracks ("Dyslexic Heart" and "Waiting for Somebody") to the grunge-tastic soundtrack of the Cameron Crowe–directed film *Singles.*

While the scene was mourning the loss of Hüsker Dü and the Mats in the mid-'90s, another crop of bands was bubbling under the surface at places like 7th St. Entry and the basement of Extreme Noise Records. In one direction, you had a political-minded rapper named **Slug**, who was one-half (along with producer **Ant**) of the indie hip-hop group **Atmosphere**. Slug's rhymes were like the lyrical equivalent of Norman Rockwell paintings—slices of life, though often reeling with themes of depression and destruction. While Atmosphere climbed the ranks, both regionally and nationally, it inspired other MCs from the Twin Cities like **Brother Ali**, **Eyedea & Abilities**, and **P.O.S.**, all of which signed to the duo's Rhymesayers Entertain-

* Unsure of the Replacements influence on today's music scene? Check out the documentary *Bastards of Young*, named for the Mats song off the band's 1995 album *Tim*, which outlines the NYC/NJ basement that launched the careers of Midtown, the Starting Line, and Armor for Sleep. Natch!

ment, a record label responsible for supporting and fostering local hip-hop talent.

Slug (real name Sean Daley) wasn't just a hip-hop head, though. He was a true fan of Minneapolis music, especially the band **Lifter Puller**. (In fact, he was so taken by them that he penned a song called "Lift Her Pull Her" on his band's Epitaph debut *Seven's Travels* and offered up guest vocals on the alt-rock band's song "Math Is Money.") Led by frontman Craig Finn, LFTR PLLR (as they were known to their diehard fans) was a thinking man's rock band fueled by angular riffs, innovative instrumentation, and often-elaborate lyrics. Unfortunately, many outside of the Twin Cities failed the IQ prerequisite, and the band threw in the towel by the turn of the century. Finn relocated to Brooklyn and reemerged with a new band, **the Hold Steady**, which carries on much of the lyrical tradition of Lifter Puller but trades art-house aesthetics for classic-rock revivalism.

As Minneapolis ushered in the Aughties,* the scene also embraced a whole new crop of bands that were making locals proud. First up was **Har Mar Superstar**†—a blend of R&B and electroclash—whose brain trust Sean Tillmann (who looks like Ron Jeremy's slightly autistic younger brother) often performs in nothing but a pair of dingy tighty whities or, if he's feeling festive, a pair of fringed, ass-less chaps. No wonder the guy's an international sex symbol. Just don't accuse him of being a one-trick pony, because Tillman's quite serious about his straight-up indie band **Sean Na Na**—so serious, in fact, that he actually wears clothes for those performances. **Motion City Soundtrack**, on the other hand, stays away from shtick because its heartfelt power-pop songs are powerful enough on their own. Since forming over a decade ago, MCS has become local music royalty, thanks to relentless touring, unwavering hometown pride, and

---

* *n.* The decade from 2000 to 2009. Yeah, I think it looks weird, too.

† Sean Tillmann actually took his namesake from the HarMar Mall, which is located in Roseville, Minnesota. Feel free to pay homage by shaking your money maker in front of the Dress Barn here.

clap-along anthems like "Future Freaks Me Out" and "Everything Is Alright."

Finally, one of the newest bands to spark a chord with the Pitchfork crowd is **Tapes 'n Tapes**, which burst onto the blog scene in 2005 with their debut album *The Loon*. These former Carleton College students play good ol' neo-psychedelic college rock, which is a far cry from the slick pop-punk sound of other up-and-comers like **Sing It Loud** and **Camera Can't Lie**, or the more hardcore-infused **Four Letter Lie**.

LABEL CONSCIOUS

It's safe to say that there would be no Minneapolis rock scene without the city's highly revered **Twin/Tone Records**. The label existed from 1977 to 1994 and was run by scenesters Peter Jesperson, Paul Stark, Charley Hallman, and Chris Osgood, whom many credit as being the fathers of the Minneapolis scene. During its seventeen-year existence, Twin/Tone was responsible for picking up on then-unknown local talent like **the Replacements**, **Babes in Toyland**, **the Jayhawks**, and **Soul Asylum**, and putting out some of their first releases (many of which were on—*gasp!*—cassette tapes). With the help of bands like **Lifter Puller**, New Hope, and Pennsylvania's **Ween** the label continued to release a smattering of albums toward the end of the '90s before finally closing its door. Twin/Tone eventually licensed material to Restless Records, part of Rykodisc, but if you go to the label's website (http://www.twintone.com), you can order custom burns of its back catalog. Although not exactly active, the Twin/Tone legacy is far from over: In 2008, fans rejoiced when Rhino Records reissued expanded versions of the Replacement's early Twin/Tone releases *Sorry Ma, Forgot to Take Out the Trash*, the *Stink* EP, *Hootenanny*, and *Let It Be*. Color me impressed!

ALMOST FAMOUS

In the music world, there's a huge division between those who rock the stage and those who stand on the side of it, furiously scribbling illegible chicken scratch on a notepad. The latter (often male, awkward in movement, and possessing the wardrobe of an overgrown eight-year-old) are known as "rock critics" and are truly a breed unto their own. They know Billy Bragg's solo catalog by heart, can rattle off the name of any band that recorded at Electric Audio, and, oddly enough, have probably spent a good amount of time lurking around the record stores and dive bars of Minneapolis.

Why is the Mill City such a hot spot for rock critic activity? Good question. Maybe it's the brisk weather or the scene's rich music history—or possibly because a Google search for "record stores + Minneapolis" delivers more than six thousand results. However, with my help, I'll provide you with the tools so you can spot rock critics at fifteen feet and properly skirt a long-winded conversation with them about the World/Inferno Friendship Society LP they just bought on eBay. After all, those who can, play an instrument; those who can't, critique—and, eventually, hate—music.

YOU CAN TELL SOMEONE'S A ROCK CRITIC IF HE IS _____.

MALE

I'm not trying to be sexist or anything, but it's true. A study conducted by the Rockism Institute of Gender Research[*] in 2005 even

---

[*] There is no such thing as the Rockism Institute of Gender Research. I totally made that up to sound really well-supported and stuff. However, I'm pretty sure that if such an institute existed, it would've come up with numbers very close to my imaginary ones.

concluded that over 85 percent of all rock critics, in fact, possess XY chromosomes. You can't argue with science. Sure, there are a handful of well-respected female rock critics (like Melissa Maerz, current senior editor at *Rolling Stone* and former music editor at the Minneapolis/St. Paul *City Pages*), but they're definitely in the minority. Yes, the rock criticism sect is another boys' club. *Shocker.*

ROCKING A MINIMAL (AND OFTENTIMES ILL-FITTING) WARDROBE

Despite being surrounded by fashionable and stylish rock stars, rock critics can hardly be described as being "fashionable" or "stylish." Instead, their wardrobe is filled with a hodgepodge of free giveaways, thrift-store pieces, and random hand-me-downs. To be specific, their uniform usually consists of the following:

* **Crew Neck T-Shirt**

  The tee is surely plastered with the name of some band or record label and has been sent gratis by some publicist, manager, label rep, or aspiring band member. Sizing is no obstacle because, let's face it, a free T-shirt is a free T-shirt.

* **Jeans**

  You can tell how much rock critics make per word by taking a gander at their denim of choice: If they're rocking G-Star Raw or A.P.C., which run upward of two hundred dollars, business is booming. However, if they're sporting a pair of Mossimo turbine gray jeans from Target or threadbare old Levi's with gaping holes in the knees, they probably haven't scored a byline in quite a while.

* **Converse All Star High-Tops**

  The standard color is black with white laces, but more flamboyant types go for red or pink. The lifespan of a pair of Chuck Taylors for regular folk is probably a year. The lifespan of a pair of Chuck Taylors for a rock critic is infinite—or until the sole wears out thinner than a piece of paper. Whichever happens first.

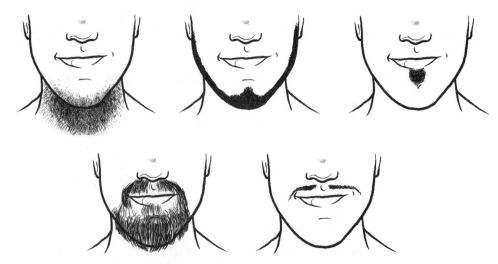

CONSTANTLY PLAGUED BY A PRESENCE OF FACIAL HAIR—OR CONSTANTLY TRYING TO GROW FACIAL HAIR (THOUGH OFTEN UNSUCCESSFULLY).

Rock critics aren't that concerned with physical appearance (as they illustrate by allowing themselves to leave their apartments looking like they do), but they do have an Achilles' heel when it comes to outward appearances: facial hair. Being able to grow it is a visible trophy for any rock critic, especially those who look like they have yet to go through puberty despite being in their early to mid-twenties. Those who are follicly challenged will often try different methods to induce growth, like shaving at least twice a day or smearing Rogaine all over their jaw line. Therefore, if you're next to a guy with a patchy neck beard who smells like a spicy flower garden, don't panic. He's not a possible target from *To Catch a Predator.* He's probably just a rock critic trying to grow a decent goatee.

EXHIBITING SYMPTOMS OF APHEPHOBIA, THE FEAR OF BEING TOUCHED

As a whole, rock critics aren't the buffest dudes on the block. They don't have gym memberships, and they definitely don't play sports. Hell, they don't even *watch* sports. They're fragile flowers who often bruise easily, which is why you won't find them venturing anywhere near the front of the stage to review a sold-out show. Instead, rock critics are content to lurk in corners or skulk at the bar, anything to avoid being touched or manhandled by sweaty, overweight Hatebreed fans or overzealous, crying tweens at a Miley Cyrus concert. That's why personal bubbles were invented, right?

HOW MUCH IS TOO MUCH?

If there are two things Sotans[*] are serious about, it's their music scene and alcohol: The Replacements were known as much for their hard-drinking lifestyle as their music. (Bassist Tommy Stinson even revealed his love for 100-proof vodka on ice in an infamous 1986 *Creem* magazine interview. Yummers!) The Hold Steady has unleashed an arsenal of alcohol-inspired rockers like "Citrus" and "Your Little Hoodrat Friend" and, of course, let's not forget Motion City Soundtrack, whose members became the heroes of frat brothers everywhere when they penned "L.G. Fuad," which translates to "Let's Get Fucked Up and Die."

Looks like, at one point or another, all great Twin Cities bands have sung about tossing back a drink—or ten. So how do you know whether these boozy bands are casual drinkers with an undying thirst for hyperbole or are in need of a twelve-step program?[†] The following quiz should help shed some light on the subject.

1. When you wake up in the morning, the first thing you crave is:
   a. Orange juice.
   b. Red Bull.
   c. Cranberry juice, but with a splash of vodka. Okay, more than a splash. Let's say a healthy pour. . . . And not a lot of cran-

---

* *n.* Term of endearment for anyone from Minnesota.

† Warning: The author of this book is in no way trivializing or making light of substance abuse. Alcoholism is no joke, so if you or someone you know might be suffering from it, please call the Drug and Alcohol Rehab Resource Center at 800-784-6776. Just like Scarlett Johansson's singing career and Jackie Stallone's astrology readings, this quiz should not be taken seriously. Oh, and if you're under twenty-one, you can skip this section altogether. I'd hate to plant a seed and have you water it with vodka or something.

berry juice. Actually, you can cut the cranberry juice altogether.

2. On a typical day, how many alcoholic beverages do you consume when you are drinking?
    a. None.
    b. 1 to 3.
    c. Wait . . . There are days when people *don't* drink? Weird. [*Long pause.*] Sorry, what was the question again? I had to do a keg stand real quick.

3. Do you have a high tolerance for alcohol?
    a. No.
    b. Sorta.
    c. Yup, I find my alcohol *highly* tolerable. Get it? *Tolerable*? *Tolerance*? Where's the nearest open-mic night? My shit is funny.

4. Do you encounter withdrawal symptoms—like nausea, hallucinations, and irritability—if you haven't had alcohol?
    a. No.
    b. Sometimes.
    c. I'll let you know as soon as I finish ralphing. . . . And that purple dinosaur in the corner stops staring at me.

ANSWER KEY

If you answered **mostly As**, you're either straight edge or have absolutely no social life. Loosen up, dude. *Geez . . .*

If you answered **mostly Bs**, then you're totally middle-of-the-road. Sometimes you feel like a drink and sometimes you don't, Almond Joy-style. Luckily for you, the closest you're going to get to rehab is by watching *Intervention* on A&E.

D.A.R.E.

TO RESIST DRUGS AND VIOLENCE.

If you answered **mostly Cs**, congrats! You're a total alkie—and probably the lead singer of a Twin Cities–based rock band. However, before you grab a mini-keg and cue up the *SingStar*, keep this in mind: If a production crew is taping you for a seemingly innocuous "documentary about substance abuse," there's a good chance that you might already be shooting footage for a future episode of *Intervention*. Don't freak out if the next door you open has all of your family inside along with an older gentleman suffering from male pattern baldness. That's Dr. Jeff VanVonderen, and he's there to help.

PUB CRAWL

Whether you're looking to connect with Minneapolis' pub-tastic history or you just wanna get driz-zunk, I'd recommend you take a scenic pub crawl—er, walking tour of the scene's finest bar establishments.

You'll want to start off at the site of **Jay's Longhorn Bar (14 S 5th St.)**, which was a punk Mecca back in the day. Often called the Midwest's CBGB—minus the gnarly bathrooms and the bar's overwhelming smell of urine—the space hosted local bands like Hüsker Dü and the Replacements, in addition to then up-and-coming acts like Talking Heads and Naked Raygun. Jay's changed hands and briefly became **Zoogie's Bar,**[*] a half-punk, half-gay club, but it didn't last and eventually closed. The address is currently host to a parking garage that sort of looks like the Guggenheim. You won't find any alcohol here (unless you bring a flask with you), but that's okay. Close your eyes and breathe in the smell of brewskies past. Ah, can't you feel the magic? Okay, enough of that new-age crap, time to book it to the next venue.

Go north on Fifth Street and then swing a left on First Avenue North until you come to **First Avenue and 7th St. Entry (701 1st Ave. N)**. The smaller side entrance is for the Entry, a dingy concert venue and watering hole for local scenesters. Sure the place is a dive now, but back in 1937, the location originally stood as a Greyhound Bus Depot and was an art-deco masterpiece. Today, instead of selling bus tickets, the club boasts two-dollar PBR tallboys from 8:00 to 11:00 p.m. each night there's a show, which is, like, *every* night. Score!

Once you're done, finish your drink and hoof it back up First Avenue to Sixth Street North and swing a left. Then take another left at Second Avenue North and you'll be looking at what is now the parking lot outside the Target Center (654 2nd Ave. N). If you take a trip in the way-back machine, though, this very cement spot housed the infamous Dü and Mats hangout **Goofy's Upper Deck**. The watering hole was located on the second floor of a skanky strip club, but the booze was cheap and the shows were kick-ass. A lot of great bands have played—and drunk—here, so you might want to take a sec and pay your respect.

When you're done, you're gonna want to hail a cab or zip up your parka for a two-mile walk to **the Red Dragon (2116 Lyndale Ave. S)**, known equally for having the best cocktails—and worst food—in the city. Its tropical drinks are super-cheap but super-potent, so remember the old adage: Beer before liquor, never sicker. For the sake of this pub crawl, let's gonna stick to beer, which makes the Dragon's three-

* Zoogie's Bar did leave its mark on the Minneapolis scene, though, by spawning one of the Replacements' first-known audience tapes. The thirty-four-song (yes . . . *thirty-four* effing songs) set took place sometime in 1981 and included covers of "Substitute" by the Who and "All Day and All of the Night" by the Kinks.

dollar domestic brews music to our ears. Assuming you've safely avoided getting sick—on either the drinks or the chewy beef chow mein*—it's time to tote your cookies to the last stop on this booze cruise.

Head south three blocks to the corner of Twenty-sixth Street and Lyndale Avenue South and you'll come upon the infamous **C.C. Club (2600 Lyndale Ave. S)**. Motion City Soundtrack's Justin Pierre immortalized the club in the song "Better Open the Door." (Sample lyric: "Frank fails to see the humor in my sad attempts at break dancing in every bar along Lyndale Avenue / Liz likes to liquor up my thoughts, from the C.C. Club to the Triple Rock.") If Pierre wasn't across the street at **Mortimer's (2001 Lyndale Ave. S)**, he was spending many a drunken night closing down C.C.'s, which only lends to the bar's credibility as a neighborhood mainstay. If you're not opposed to partaking in a boot-and-rally,† I'd tell you to give the steak and eggs a chance. But, if you're more interested in maintaining a liquid diet, then order an eight-dollar pitcher.

I hope my lil' pub crawl offered up some scenic spots to get your drink on. Now there's only one thing left to do after docking the booze cruise, and that's board the snooze cruise. *Arrrr*, matey!

---

* I tried to warn you.

† *n.* Slang. The act of drinking a lot of booze, blowing chunks, and then continuing to drink more booze.

MAPPING OUT THE TWIN CITIES

CLICHÉ (2403 LYNDALE AVE. S, MINNEAPOLIS, MN 55405; HTTP://WWW.CLICHEMPLS.COM)

Minnesota natives (and married co-owners) Joshua and Delayna Sundberg opened this cutting-edge boutique in hopes of celebrating local designers, and by the look of the super-cute merchandise and window displays, I'd say mission accomplished. Not only do the Sundbergs support the scene specializing in Minnesotan-made goods, but the couple also hosts monthly events ranging from art to runway shows.

ELECTRIC FETUS (2000 4TH AVE. S, MINNEAPOLIS, MN 55404; HTTP://WWW.ELECTRICFETUS.COM)

It's hard to believe that despite the influx of Best Buys and CD Warehouses, the Electric Fetus has managed to remain a Minneapolis record store staple for over forty years. Much like San Francisco's Amoeba Music, the Fetus is stacked with music from floor to ceiling. It's even been estimated that the store holds over fifty thousand titles, including hard-to-find vinyl, import CDs, box sets, and various clothing and accessories. The store even publishes its own newsletter, *The Chord*, which offers new release info, employee picks, and coupons.

What makes scenesters overlook the horrendous moniker and cherish the Fetus is the fact that the store also has a distribution company called Onestop that provides CDs to other local and independent record stores. What does this mean? Well, say you're in a baby band called the Autumn Coronary and you just recorded your first album, called *I'm Bleeding, It's Cold Out*. You're so stoked for people to hear your unique blend of math-rock/pop-punk/jazz fusion but you're still unsigned and have no idea how to get stores to stock your CD. Enter Onestop, which will distribute your album on consignment. Now when your mother asks you where she can buy a copy of your record, you can tell her, "Electric Fetus, Ma!" (Just be sure to clarify that it's a record store and not some kind of pro-life action league.)

EXTREME NOISE RECORDS (407 W LAKE ST., MINNEAPOLIS, MN 55408; HTTP://WWW.EXTREMENOISE.COM)

Unlike other record stores, Extreme Noise is a punk-rock cooperative run exclusively by volunteers. All proceeds from CDs, records, tapes, T-shirts, spikes, and 'zines are reinvested into the store and local punk projects. The co-op boasts one of the world's largest punk inventories, although beware: Extreme Noise does not mail order. Alas, those suffering from agoraphobia will just have to make do with whatever Anal Blast album they can find on Amazon.

FIFTH ELEMENT (2411 HENNEPIN AVE., MINNEAPOLIS, MN 55405; HTTP://WWW.FIFTHELEMENTONLINE.COM)

For those getting their headlines from AllHipHop.com instead of AbsolutePunk.net, there isn't a better record store than Fifth Element. Opened in 1999 by Rhymesayers Entertainment, the shop hosts a huge inventory of CDs, DVDs, clothing, and comics by classic and modern hip-hop artists, but goes above and beyond in showcasing material by local artists like Brother Ali, Atmosphere, and Eyedea & Abilities.

PIZZA LUCÉ (2200 E FRANKLIN AVE., MINNEAPOLIS, MN 55404; HTTP://WWW.PIZZALUCE.COM)

In the years since the joint opened in 1993, both Citysearch.com and *City Pages* readers have voted Pizza Lucé as having *the* best pizza in the 612 area code. What makes this pie so special? Four words: garlic mashed potato pizza. Yeah, you heard me. This white pizza is topped by a starchy—yet savory—combo of red mashed potatoes, garlic butter, tomatoes, green onion, and feta cheese. Sure, even a small sliver sits like a brick in your stomach, but it's worth every bite.

If you're a carb Nazi, no worries. Indulge in one of Lucé's endless salads and bask in the glory of past employees. Over the years, Pizza Lucé has remained a loyal employer to many of the scene's best and brightest bands—like Motion City's Josh Cain and Jesse Johnson, plus various members of now-defunct bands like the Stereo, Cadillac Blindside, and Claire de Lune—because it was one of the city's few establishments that would keep jobs open while bands hit the road to tour. Order from any of Lucé's four Twin Cities locations and you never know which past, present, or future scenester is going to deliver your pizzas!

SEWARD COMMUNITY CAFÉ (2129 E FRANKLIN AVE., MINNEAPOLIS, MN 55404; HTTP://WWW.SEWARDCAFEMPLS.NET)

Much like Extreme Noise Records, Seward Community Café has been owned and operated by community volunteers since 1974. Not only does the café cater to local tastes, but it also supports local, independent, and organic products whenever possible. During the growing season, the kitchen even tries to incorporate as much produce as possible from the Common Harvest CSA (Community Supported Agriculture). Impressed yet? You ain't seen nothing until you try the Super Red Green Earth breakfast platter.

TERMINAL BAR (409 E HENNEPIN AVE., MINNEAPOLIS, MN 55414; HTTP://WWW.MYSPACE.COM/TERMINALBARMUSIC)

Terminal Bar separates itself from the pack by offering stuff what other establishments don't: beer nuts, Slim Jims, aspirin, and, most important, free popcorn. Sure, some Sotans refer to Terminal Bar as "Urinal Bar" because of the overwhelming smell emanating from the men's bathroom, but that doesn't stop scenesters from coming in droves to pack this place nightly. Just make sure to run to the ATM before you meet your peeps because this bar's cash only.

TREEHOUSE RECORDS (2557 LYNDALE AVE. S, MINNEAPO-LIS, MN 55405)

Music, music, and more music—that pretty much describes what you'll find inside Treehouse Records. Treehouse opened its doors in 2001 after a long line of record stores occupied the corner of Twenty-Sixth and Lyndale Avenue. (The most famous of which was Oarfolkjokeopus Records,* which christened the space back in 1972.) Today, Treehouse is like heaven for vinyl collectors, offering an obscene number of LPs and 45s, in addition to tons of new and used CDs. Don't forget to turn off your cell phone before entering this music sanctuary unless you wanna get the boot.

TRIPLE ROCK SOCIAL CLUB (629 CEDAR AVE. S, MINNEAP-OLIS, MN 55454; HTTP://WWW.TRIPLEROCKSOCIALCLUB .COM)

When the Triple Rock Social Club opened its doors in 1998, it was the one of the first bars in the Twin Cities that was owned and operated by one of the scene's own—Dillinger Four's Erik Funk and his wife, Gretchen—and it quickly became anything *but* your typical punk dive. This bar was made *by* musicians *for* musicians and you could tell, from the eclectic selection on the jukebox (which included everything from Johnny Cash to Negative Approach) to the people tending bar (you can still catch Dillinger guitarist/vocalist Billy Morrisette slinging cocktails on the regular).

Five years later, the Triple Rock added a stage and quickly transformed into a much-needed all-ages, mid-sized venue. The venue opened on a weekend in June 2003, and included shows by Lifter Puller, the Mountain Goats, the Oranges Band, and the Crush. Today, the venue remains one of the Twin Cities' best places to see live music, not to mention some amazing comedians (like Paul F. Tompkins and Doug Stanhope) and book readings (Chuck Palahniuk and Anthony

---

* After exactly forty-seven days of nonstop research, I was unable to find out the definition for "Oarfolkjokeopus." If you happen to know what the name means, feel free to school my tired ass!

THE TWIN CITIES

Bourdain, anyone?). Many credit the Triple Rock—and the members of Dillinger Four—for solidifying the Twin Cities music scene and I'd totally have to agree. Looking for more proof? Then listen to the following musical homages, which all name-check the venue: "Seeing Double at the Triple Rock" by NOFX, "Better Open the Door" by Motion City Soundtrack, and "Home (Is Where the Van Is)" by Limbeck.

A MOMENT OF SILENCE

PROFANE EXISTENCE (P.O. BOX 18051, MINNEAPOLIS, MN 55418; HTTP://WWW.PROFANEEXISTENCE.COM)

Profane Existence is the stuff that anarchist dreams are made of: Part fanzine, part record label, part activist organization, PE was *all* about spreading the anarcho-punk gospel. The collective was started in 1989 by a bunch of local punkers who wanted the scene to be more politically minded and soon evolved into a platform for then-unknown writers, poets, and crust-punk* bands to get their message across. The label sector first made waves for releasing the only full-length album by Nausea, NYC's premiere crust band, and continued to put out releases by bands like Misery, Doom, Anarcrust, and Counterblast. On the literary side of things, PE released forty issues of their own free, self-titled 'zine, which offered articles on topics from veganism to the antifascist movement and everything in between. C'mon, what anarcho-punk doesn't want to read an interview with Nuclear Assault *and* learn about the best places to get vegan Indian food?

In 1998, after almost ten years of throwing a middle finger to the Man, Profane Existence threatened extinction and then the collective folded, closing the storefront but keeping the distribution end of

---

* *n.* A subgenre of music defined by powerful metal riffs, lots of distortion, and lyrics about subjects like nuclear war and death. "Crusty" bands are usually comprised of a bunch of pudgy, long-haired guys from England (or Sweden) who look like they haven't showered since 1980—though that's probably being generous. See any band whose members still wear a Crass patch on their sleeveless jean jackets.

things running. In 2000, PE put on its combat boots once again to revive the label and 'zine. With a new slogan ("Making punk a threat again, bitches!"*); new grindcore, thrash, black metal, and crust bands (like Murder Disco Experience and Warcopolis); and a new batch of issues to tackle (damn, where do I start?), Profane Existence seemed stronger and more active than ever—until it was announced on July 16, 2008, that the label would stop production on all releases that weren't already in the manufacturing process. The decision came a year shy of the label's twenty-year anniversary and only two months after PE became "the punk world's first member-supported independent media cooperative." (I wasn't sure what that meant, but it sounded pretty impressive.)

---

* Okay, I added the "bitches" part because I thought it sounded super tough. The real slogan is just "Making punk a threat again." Feel free to add the "bitches" for emphasis, though.

I hope you enjoyed your journey. Just think of all the places you've gone and the scenes you've visited—all without spending a penny on gas. (You can thank me for that later.) With tons of insider information, tips, and tricks, I hope that you walk away from this fabulous book with a greater understanding of and respect for your favorite bands. If you're lucky enough to live in one of the eleven scenes you just read about, I hope you'll take to the streets and truly discover everything your surroundings have to offer. If you're stuck in Crib Death, Iowa, then I recommend you update your Travelocity FareWatcher tout de suite so you can experience live and in person all the good stuff we've been talking about.

Plus, always remember: If you're given a choice on how to explore your favorite music communities, be sure to take the scenic route.

I would like to thank my editor, Jeremy Cesarec, at HarperCollins for going above and beyond the call of duty by being my second set of eyes, creative sounding board, *and* part-time therapist. I would also like to thank my amazing agents, Anne Garrett and Jim Fitzgerald, for believing in my wild style, being my biggest cheerleaders, and wearing more hats than Bartholomew Cubbins. (That reference is for you, dad.) Speaking of, I credit my parents—Eileen and Jeff Simon—with single-handedly keeping me sane throughout the entire writing process. If not for their love and encouragement, I would still be sitting in front of a blank laptop screen, terrified and surrounded by a mountain of empty Diet Coke cans. Then there's my brother from another mother, Trevor Kelley. Your creative brilliance is only matched by your keen fashion sense, both of which will always be an inspiration to me.

Unlimited amounts of hugs and kisses also go to Rob Dobi, Bridget Gibbons, John Millin, Regan Rose, and Pedro; Linsey Molloy, Jessica Weeks, Lesley Federman, Kate Cafaro, Brian Bumbery, Gurj Bassi, Marilyn Curtiss, Jennifer Curtiss, Neil Rubenstein, Mike Dubin, Josh Cain, Sara Newens, Phil Huffman, Sarah Lewitinn, and Karen Ruttner; Kermit Carter and the

Acknowledgments

Triple Rock Social Club; Carrie Kania and everyone at HarperCollins; Joan Hiller, wiL Francis, Jonah Bayer, Debbie Wunder and Rusty Pistachio; Teeter Sperber, Angie St. Louis and Emmy Lou; Rachel Lux, Kerri Borsuk, Aaron Wilson and Norman Wonderly; Chad Gilbert, Chris Carrabba, Chad Johnson and Tooth & Nail; Libby Henry, Annie Shapiro and Steven Smith at Fuse; Amy Welsh, Jenny Reader and Victory Records; Chris Farinas, Matt Galle, John Janick and Fueled by Ramen Records; Kevin Lyman, Sarah Baer and Kate Truscott at 4Fini; T. Cole Rachel, Dave Hansen, Austin Griswold and Epitaph Records; Craig Kallman, Julie Greenwald, Livia Tortella, Chris Foitle, Mollie Moore, Glenn Fukushima and everyone at Atlantic Records; Dan Suh, Keith Buckley, Heidi Anne-Noel, Riley Breckenridge, Jason Tate and AbsolutePunk.net.

Finally, I would like to send a hundred tons of gratitude to my amazing team at Buzznet. Thank you for rescuing me from those glacial Cleveland winters and for encouraging me to dream big. That means you, Tyler Goldman, Marc Brown, Scott Boyd, Brad Barrish, Jeff Leeds, Karen Hart, Chris Tragos, Alan Citron, Bree McGuire, Richard Flores, and Mark Oshiro.

ALSO BY LESLIE SIMON AND TREVOR KELLEY

EVERYBODY HURTS
An Essential Guide to Emo Culture

ISBN 978-0-06-119539-6
(paperback)

Leslie Simon and Trevor Kelley lead the reader through the world of emo including its ideology, music, and fashion, as well as its influences on film, television, and literature. With a healthy dose of snark and sarcasm, EVERYBODY HURTS uses diagrams, illustrations, timelines, and step—by—step instructions to help the reader successfully achieve the ultimate emo lifestyle. Or, alternately, teach him to spot an emo kid across the mall in order to mock him mercilessly.

"A smart, funny and revealing book that's pretty much a must read for kids in the scene."

—Chris Carrabba, DASHBOARD CONFESSIONAL